CREATIVE HIRING

THE PINNACLE MODEL *for* SPONTANEOUS, IMAGINATIVE, COLLABORATIVE INTERVIEWS

A practical guide for modern **recruiters and **hiring managers***

Ozan Dagdeviren

All rights reserved. No part of this publication may be reproduced, distributed, or transmitted in any form or by any means, including photocopying, recording, or other electronic or mechanical methods, without the prior written permission of the publisher, except in the case of brief quotations embodied in critical reviews and certain other noncommercial uses permitted by copyright law.

Although every precaution has been taken to verify the accuracy of the information contained herein, the author and publisher assume no responsibility for any errors or omissions.

Copyright © 2015 by Ozan Dagdeviren

First Edition: September 2015

ISBN: 978-1517138080

Dedicated to all those who work for a living...

...and to those who work for causes above themselves.

CONTENTS

- INTRODUCTION 9
- PART ONE: THE THEORY 15
- Why *Talent Recruitment* is the Most Important Job in any Organization 16
- The Basic Problems of Recruitment and the Need for a New Model 27
- Understanding Traditional Interview Models 42
- Long-Neglected Candidate Psychology 62
- PART TWO: THE PRACTICE 69
- The Pinnacle Model and the Solution Proposition 71
- The Ascent - Principle 1: Enable Mental Comfort 79
- The Ascent - Principle 2: Earn Respect 92
- The Ascent - Principle 3: Surprise (or Pattern Break) 103
- The Pinnacle - Principle 4: Show Genuine Interest 117
- The Descent - Principle 5: Side with the Candidate 131
- The Descent - Principle 6: Know Yourself 144
- The Descent - Principle 7: Let Them Know 156
- Skill Building for Interviewers 169
- CONCLUSION 173
- HAND GUIDE & Summary of Key Takeaways 178
- WORKS CITED 186

INTRODUCTION

This book is a tool to make lasting human connections that enable precise analyses and generation of unique insights. It is a tool to see the hidden motivations, hesitations, beliefs, fears, ambitions, thoughts, questions, values and personality characteristics of the people we meet. It's a unified theory of in-depth human interaction that can be used both in and out of the business setting.

The initial purpose of this work is to guide the recruiters and hiring managers of an organization towards better hiring decisions through increasing the quality of their interview practices and improving the candidate experience. However, in addition to this purpose, the theory and practice provided here is found to be beneficial and applicable in any similar business setting which holds similar human interaction dynamics. Its benefits can go beyond recruiting, and the ideas and tips here can be utilized in broader application areas such as sales; purchasing; marketing or simply any context a human related business decision making takes place. Simply put, the model and its theory can be used to solve, understand and get better at any one-on-one, face-to-face dialogue between people.

The Pinnacle Model introduced hereon is a unique perspective founded on the theory and dynamics of human thinking, feeling and acting. It is shaped with respect to the candidate psychology before, during and after the interview and aims to push the evolution of the job interview into a *mutually enjoyable learning and improvement opportunity for the candidate and the recruiter or hiring manager*. Most importantly it aims to accomplish this while enabling the evaluator to see behind the mask of business formality and decipher the motivations and competencies of the candidate with a high degree of precision.

The model is theorized by a combination of some key disciplines. I have been lucky enough to gain an academic education at reputable institutions in the disciplines of Sociology, Psychology and

Communication Studies on one hand, and field experience in recruitment practice on the other. During this time I have had the opportunity to work in mid-level professional and chief-level executive recruitment projects mainly in the technology sector, conducting around three thousand individual interviews getting to know all colors of the human character. This model owes its existence to this unique perspective that is a result of coinciding theory and practice. It is a culmination of academic knowledge as well as business acumen.

To be clear, as the core aim of this work is to introduce and globally popularize The Pinnacle Model, I offer you, the reader a choice. If you are not curious about the theory and simply looking for practical insights, or too excited to know more about the model itself, consider starting from *PART TWO: The Practice*. Here you can discover some central ideas regarding the interview and find practical examples, tips, suggestions…

If you are the type of person who likes to see the full picture before going into details; if you are interested in understanding the social and psychological dynamics of the interview and gain a thorough understanding that reaches beyond applicable suggestions, I strongly suggest you start from the beginning.

At the end of each chapter under *The Practice*, you will find a concise list of *Key Takeaways*. These pointers serve as a reference to central ideas communicated in each principle to facilitate remembering what each part is really about at a quick glance. They can be thought as forming the skeleton of the model. Also at the end of the book, you will find a bridged list of these pointers collected to help the reader see the model from a perspective and take notes or refer back to some points when needed. It is intended as a summary and a Hand Guide of the Pinnacle Model.

Seeing through another person gives one a significant advantage in any personal or professional confrontation. I personally believe it is the single most important lifelong skill one can develop in a society. This book is written in the hope of contributing in some measure to that development.

Let's begin the journey to the top.

PART ONE: THE THEORY

Why *Talent Recruitment* is the Most Important Job in any Organization

The biggest driving force in our modern economy is human labor. It is not natural resources, not industrial methods, not systems nor processes. In every corner of the world–albeit with gigantic differences in the levels of compensation, comfort and benefits between those who work–human labor is the very foundation on which value is created. The value being created usually varies in its range from physical to cognitive, and most jobs will have a mixture of both elements. Similarly, the dependency on the exploitation of natural resources, the amount of industrialized methods in place and the amount blue and white collar workers who rely on systems and processes vary greatly as well. A general trend seems to point out that white collar workers work in what we can characterize as more cognitive 'office jobs' that are of administrative or managerial nature as opposed to the blue collar jobs that are of a physical nature and are mainly concentrated in the manufacturing industries.

As the set of skills that are required for executing the job become more nuanced and complex, due first to the over-arching and long-time-coming trend of specialization of labor (Rosen 1983, Boserup 1981) and secondly due to the direct and indirect consequences of automation (Rifkin 1996, Grey 2015); what we shall simply call *talent* becomes an increasingly important determinant of labor performance. In turn, it becomes a key determinant in the commercial success of the organization. (Although some NGO's, similar nonprofit and charity organizations share similar qualities, it should be clear that from here on, we mainly refer to *for* profit and privately owned corporations when we use the term 'organization'. The other reason why I favor the term organization is that it is a direct reference to the fact that it is an organization of people, describing how people with different personalities, priorities and lives *organize* themselves towards a shared goal.)

The first factor, specialization of the workforce is a direct result of the overwhelming and consistent desire of organizations towards efficiency. This desire is indeed self-evident looking at the workforce today. Instead of investing in a team of five members with broad/generalist role definitions; it is more efficient to train and gain depth of expertise in the execution of each job by dividing the team's responsibility into five main domains and training each personnel for those specialized roles. The growth rate of the organization is also a crucial factor in determining the optimal rate of specialization. As the organizations grow in size and the workload increases, a general reflex seems to be to break the work down into even smaller fragments or bits of specialization. That is why organizations end up with teams which, for instance, are only responsible for a very specific type of Facebook ad campaign management and optimization, but do not have a full grasp of the overall marketing strategy and the main message (core value proposition) of the organization. This is a direct result of increasing complexity of the work. Specialization is one solution but there is a point where it becomes redundant and stops solving problems created by increasing complexity. It is certainly not the ideal or future-proof way to deal with change.

Hiring people with high levels of ability to adapt is the ideal way to deal with increasing complexity and a non-stop redefinition of the work due to new disruptive technologies and work models. This is why the ability to adapt is seen as a core competency when scouting for top talent. People who are not one-trick ponies, but can actually quickly adapt to changing work definitions and innovate with new technologies are the biggest value creators. Thus the biggest strategic assets of any organization–especially in technology related industries that have a high ratio of workers who use cognitive skills rather than physical–are its loyal and adaptive *talents* who have come together with a sense of shared purpose and meaning.

The second omnipresent trend of our economy since the early and humble beginnings of the invention of the *plow* is automation. (One can fairly argue our ability to automate aspects of life predates the invention of the plow, but this is a momentous and history changing event due to its effect on the economy and workforce as well as our agricultural production capacity back then, so let's stick with it.) With the invention of the plow and our use of domestic animals for plowing the fields, we have clearly and significantly demonstrated our ability to use the cognitive capacity we hold to extract more workforce value out of the natural environment. In essence, the robotic and digital aspects which we perceive to be synonymous with automation today are a continuation of the same story. Let's look at how it began from a somewhat reversed perspective: With the introduction of the animal drawn plow, the task of plowing a field became *easier* and *more complex* for the farmer at the same time. The dependency on manual labor has decreased while the dependency on cognitive labor increased. On the one hand, it has liberated the farmer from pulling the plow physically, adding more production value and more time. On the other hand, the increased complexity meant an increased need for time planning, route optimization for the plowing of the field, learning about better animal breeding techniques and so on… Ability to learn faster, find creative solutions, strategize and plan became factors. With them, so did what we call talent. It was now possible to look at farms in a region and determine the better planner, the better route optimizer, the better breeder. Strangely, it also became possible to draw a clear and direct correlation between the cognitive capacity and *talent* of the farmer and labor results. My point is that, this trend has always been ongoing, like an undercurrent, but not as apparent as today, when the war for talent is at its peak.

Today, competing over and retaining the best talent–the best cognitive machine that is able to see problems, improvise solutions, innovate and invent–is and should be the number one strategic priority of any organization that wishes to advance, or simply disrupt its competition rather than be made obsolete.

This should not be interpreted in a way to suggest the fixed assets of an organization; namely the facilities, the machinery and the physical devices used in the production of goods and services are useless. It is quite the opposite. These fixed assets are very valuable. The strikingly simple fact is that, their value can only be extracted to their fullest capacity with the help of competent, intelligent, motivated, dedicated and innovative people. Thus, it is an unavoidable reality of our age: The more organizations automate, the fewer people they need. The fewer people they need, they need people of higher quality and talent (Jeanne Meister C., Karie Willyerd 2010).

All the tools, processes, procedures, systems, regulations and machinery of an organization are an extension of the human body and intellect. They are identical to the plow in an effort to drive more value out of the nature and economy. Organizations are run by strategic, sub-strategic and tactical decisions made by people. The tools we create, if we use them well, are there to help us make the right decisions. They help with more data, more visualization, more comparison and an access to a wide network of experience and knowledge shared on an unimaginable global scale. At the center of it all, it has always been about people, the best leaders you can think of are the quickest to look at the working world and the human condition to see this picture with clarity. Talent is at the center of it all. Until we invent true Artificial Intelligence, technology will be an extension of our humanity, and our success will depend on the degree to which we understand and utilize it. Though, if the day of a true AI comes, role of the human element in the workforce will clearly and sharply change. We won't be the agent that uses technology for the more efficient extraction of value from nature, but rather we will reverse positions and assume a new role; as *one* of the tools used in this value creation, passing on the torch to increase the complexity, invent and innovate, to true AI.

Until that hypothetical day comes, human cognitive labor (people) is the single most important determinant in an organizations success. Talent Recruitment is the study of finding those, *the talents*.

It should be noted that creating the organizational culture and structure under which the employees can flourish and investing in employee retention strategies are still very important and critical parts of the whole, without which talent management will be incomplete.

From here on, however, our main focus will be recruitment; namely the effort to determine who actually can make the cut and join the organization. More specifically, we will focus on the job interview itself, the core, the climax and the key decision point of the recruitment process.

The Basic Problems of Recruitment and the Need for a New Model

Let's be honest here. Recruitment is problematic.

It is problematic both from the candidate's perspective; regarding the quality of the overall experience (especially the interview itself) and from the perspective of the organization; in its ability to seek out and reach the top talent. After a round of unsatisfactory dialogues between the two parties, the candidate suffers feelings akin to being left in the dark, exploited, having her time wasted or in the worst case, being unfairly judged. The organization side is not as desperate, but there is still a feeling of disappointment on the road to discovering the best talent. Candidates trigger a variety of emotions and reflexes on the part of the organization (namely the recruiters) as well, ranging from apathy to anger, especially if they end up with no tangible leads or candidates after so much time and energy investment. The good news is that it can be better, both for the recruiters and the candidates. This work is the attempt to tell how that can be.

To address these conflicts though, we have to first define and understand what recruitment is.

Recruitment can formally be defined as the functional expertise through which structured organizations manage their prospective employee search, selection, offer, onboarding & orientation processes and more recently, plan their employer branding efforts. Informally and quite simply, recruitment is how an organization decides on its hires. At the core of the recruitment effort lies the interview which is the stage for the interaction of the candidate and the recruiter or hiring manager. The recruitment process can be divided up into its major processes, let's have a look at the basic structure.

The Simplified Structure of A Recruitment Process
for Recruiters

- Understand the business **strategy**
- Build a **network** of candidates
- Develop the job **brief**
- Initiate the candidate **search**
- Assemble a **list** of good fits
- Conduct the **interview**
- **Assess** with tests, case studies, inventories and other resources
- Give and receive **feedbacks**
- Manage the **Offer** and **Onboarding**

Here are the ten steps of a generic recruitment process with more detail:

1. Understand the long term business strategy and culture of the organization.
2. Build a network of candidates that is relevant to the organization's needs (in terms of sector, know-how and culture).
3. Either receive the recruitment brief or help in its construction (determine competencies) objectives and responsibilities of the role, draw out an ideal candidate profile).
4. Initiate candidate search: Use the engaged network of candidates, use social media platforms such as Linkedin, use job boards and job adverts, conduct targeted search.
5. Evaluate the applicants or potential leads to create an interview list of fitting candidates.
6. Conduct and/or join the interview(s).
7. Conduct other tests, case studies, assessments and personality inventories as needed (either before or after interviews).
8. Give and receive the feedbacks.
9. Present the formal job offer.
10. Manage the onboarding and orientation.

As we can see there are quite a number of decision points, represented by the exclamation marks in the graphic. One of them is the search (on paper) elimination: As anyone who has ever applied for a job knows very well, not all candidates get a chance for a face to face interview. Indeed, many candidates never have their CV's inspected in detail if they don't fit the basic search criteria. In other cases however, when the candidate profile is thought to be a general fit in terms of experience, area of expertise and other general criteria, either a face to face interview or some sort of assessment for a better determination of their competencies and skill sets will follow.

Please bear in mind that this is a simplification intended to give a general idea of the process for those who are not familiar with it. There isn't a single, consistent, standardized procedure shared by all organizations. The chronology of the interview and assessments are mostly fluid, some steps are skipped, not all organizations put out job adverts all the time nor do they start with a large pool of candidates. Some put more weight on objective test scores, while others have a bigger tendency to hire for attitude and motivation. It is again very common, even in large and global organizations, to have referrals from inside the company which can speed up the process, influence decision makers or simply help the candidate clear some of the steps.

The single global constant in each hiring situation is the interview. Although assessments, tests, psychological inventories and other such tools are great for providing the decision makers with more data and support points, the central and deterministic role of the interview cannot be ignored. Looking at our times from a distance, we are witnessing the proliferation of human knowledge and creation of innovation at warp speed. Our collective neural network, the internet, has irreversibly changed the way we think about and do business. It will not stop, and our *ways* of doing business will continue to be disrupted at even a greater pace. It is possible to argue that, one day, most jobs could be automated. This is a strong argument I dare not oppose. However it is clear jobs that require in depth one-on-one dialogue and the need to truly understand another human being are last on that list. The qualities that enable us to truly connect with other people, to empathize and understand, are what define us as human beings. A machine can measure, but it can't understand. When a machine *can* understand, it is no longer a machine in the crude sense of the word we use today, but indeed a form of true AI.

Drawing from this, I believe for the coming future, the role of highly trained recruiters will be even greater in the organizations. Many parts of the recruitment process can and **will** be automated and optimized, such as keyword based CV filtration, application management and the offer process. The exception will be the interview itself, because by definition the interview requires understanding a person and making a decision. The interview will remain as the core part of a recruiter's job and her most valued skill.

The day we can confidently say that *a machine is capable of comprehensively understanding a human being*, the picture in which human judgment is essential might change; but not before.

The Interview Itself

The Interview lies at the heart of recruitment. Though it is not the only aspect of it, it is the climax of the decision process. It is where the stories of the recruiter and the candidate converge, but at the end of the day it is a bigger challenge for the candidate. All aspects of one's character come out; the passions, the indifferences, ideas, feelings, anxieties and hopes and dreams all come together. The stage is now set for the display of character. The interviewee's ideas about work and life, ideas about culture, tendencies of openness or diplomacy, feelings of self-image and all insecurities held in are now ready to be questioned, scrutinized, and challenged–both by the person herself and by the recruiter/interviewer. Yet, independent of its importance, an interview can (and occasionally does!) go wrong. It embodies complex dynamics. So let's take a step back and try to understand why and how a seemingly simple face-to-face dialogue between two or more people turns into something complex.

Believe this; our very own identity is a self-told story (Carl Rogers, Abraham Maslow 2008). Since reaching the age of self-awareness we construct an identity and strive for consistency... Who are we? Are we defined by our jobs? Are we defined by our education? Are we defined by our taste in music or vacation preferences? Or do we put familial bonds and our kinship relations before all others while talking about ourselves. Looking at our past, we omit details we don't like–or rather not face, and exaggerate the value or weight of the events and accomplishments that we think are more in line with our version of self-identity. The reality in essence, there is always a gap–a huge gap–or in other words, a *tension* between our objective, material past experiences (our factual history) and our constructed self-image (of who we think we are or wish to be). This goes very deep into the idea of the self and it is a complex philosophical discussion in its entirety. For the sake of our argument let it now suffice to say our self-image is never perfect, never complete and always under construction and restoration.

This is one reason why the interview is a complex dialogue, it is essentially about self-image. All the psychological intricacies and problems of self-representation (Harter 1998) surface here. What happens during the interview in the mind of a candidate is, with almost no exception, past events and experience (the factual) clash with the ideas of self-image (the ideal). This *tension*, the first problem of the interview, is so central and so pivotal to the dialogue taking place, it must be studied and understood more clearly if we are to move forward. Ignoring this state of mind, which is the elephant in the room, puts up a huge wall between the candidate and the recruiter. Whenever we are able to acknowledge this, we are one step closer to making a real connection and establishing a true dialogue, rather than a diplomatic one.

To put it simply, overcoming the first problem of the interview lies in understanding and being aware of this existential tension about identity and self-representation the candidate is experiencing. Also consider, even in cases where the candidate herself isn't aware of or isn't able to articulate this tension, it still exists.

Let's now go back to the moment of the interview. So the person is put face to face with the very difficult task of "talking about oneself". How does one do that exactly? How on earth do you conceptualize and talk clearly about your own thoughts and feelings–things you don't even fully understand? How do you take the most complex living thing you know from inside out, and put it through a simple, easy to understand narrative? How do you craft a story that is honest and true to yourself while keeping it clean, leaving out all the confusion and disappointments that constitute life itself? And finally, how do you embed your competencies, success stories and work accomplishments into this story while still being authentic?

It's a struggle and an almost impossible task. The only way for a recruiter or hiring manager to truly understand and decrypt the other person, is to appreciate and show empathy to this struggle and try to see the complexity of the person rather than focusing on abridging to basic concepts and keywords to simplify. From the candidate's perspective, the beginning or early half of the interview is a decision point on whether to put on a fake plastic face or to make the effort to try to be authentic. Candidates have to have the *respect* for the recruiter and a certain level of *trust* about being judged honestly, or the chance of an open dialogue is lost.

The second problem of the interview is the tension between authenticity and showcasing accomplishments. On the one hand the candidate needs to be open, humble, honest, self-confident, likeable and true to herself, while at the same time doing her best to influence, **to enchant**, to show professional and personal accomplishments, the medals and belts of honor. Most people react to this tension by choosing cold hard diplomacy, preferring political correctness and faking it, instead of authenticity. While others who decide to be themselves, feel that they risk coming across as average or worse, underachiever profiles.

So what is the solution? Is there even a solution at all? The answer is yes!

We need a new philosophy of conducting interviews that aims to achieve the *Naturally Flowing Conversation* and is based on the Seven

Founding Principles of The Pinnacle Model. But before introducing the new model it is wise to look at the existing pool of knowledge on the issue. In the following chapter, we will walk through the effectual and dominant ideas in recruiting today, with the clear intention of discovering which topics are addressed and which are underdeveloped.

Understanding Traditional Interview Models

It is worth repeating here; the aim of this book is not to define what the timing, format or the structure of an interview should be. It is also clearly not a guide on the very basic techniques of an interview, such as letting the candidate speak, not interrupting right after a question, following up with in depth questions, making eye contact, learning to tolerate silences and such... Many professionals in this practice should already have this depth of information. There are a lot of rich resources, too. Irving Seidman's guide for *Interviewing as Qualitative Research*, albeit a bit dated, includes great insights. *Who: The A Method for Hiring*-by Geoff Smart and Randy Street is also an essential read.

This book assumes and even expects a basic understanding of how an interview works. The aim here is to show a model for transcending the elementary do's and don'ts of conducting an interview.

But still, to make sure we are all on the same page let's do some research and have a look at the existing ideas, models and theories used around recruiting and interviewing today. What would a recruiter looking for sources to improve her professional skills find? By answering this, we can sketch a rough map of the knowledge accumulated around recruitment and interviewing techniques.

The Situation As It Is

The first idea we will discover pertains to the structure of the interview. Broadly, interviews can be classified as a) unstructured, b) structured and c) semi-structured. An **unstructured** or non-directive interview is an interview style in which questions are not prearranged (Blackman 2002). It resembles a free-flowing conversation and might be used to gain a general idea about the subject. These are also named *discovery interviews* (more frequently in qualitative and quantitative research). The unstructured interview is considered the polar opposite of the structured interview in which all questions to be asked in the interview are predetermined. The main advantage of the unstructured nature of the interview lies in the fact that it creates a more natural environment under which the interviewer and interviewee contribute together to the conversation. Therefore it is thought to create valuable information through spontaneous interaction. Bagele Chilisa (2011) explains the functioning of the unstructured interview in a concise way. Albeit in the different context of anthropological research, Chilisa's point can be applied to the job interview: *"[The neutral environment] gives the unstructured interview an advantage over the structured interview in that it produces more reliable information and may enable the interview subject to bring forward experiences and knowledge that the interviewer had not previously considered. Each unstructured depends on the interviewer and interviewee together to create knowledge, and therefore the characteristics of the interview can vary from one conversation to another."*

The disadvantage, when structure is wholly lacking, can be the difficulty in diverting the conversation to focus on the most important topics. The relaxed nature of the interview also means little to no preparation on the interviewee's part and the level of challenge is fairly low. As we will discuss in more detail, the interviewee must feel a certain level of tolerable pressure to concentrate and perform (so must the interviewer). This is difficult to achieve in the unstructured interview. Another disadvantage is, unstructured interviews are hard to fit into pre-determined time slots as the case usually is for the average business day. Due to its free-form nature, the key content needed to evaluate the candidate might still be lacking after a full hour of conversation.

The structured interview on the other hand has the benefits of using pre-prepared questions that take direct stabs at the topic, have very predictable timings, remove the element of the subjectivity of the interviewer and create standardization (that in turn makes possible compare answers) between the candidates. These kind of interviews are good at neutral topics of discussion–on topics that the interviewee feels no pressure when telling the truth–such as their favorite team or what they think about the recently built public park. Thus they are frequently referred to in quantitative research methods and questionnaires. However, in more delicate or personal matters, this approach loses the edge due to its robotic nature. Talking about one's self, personality, future desires and past mistakes is a very private and sensitive matter. As such it requires the agency and *involvement* of another individual who will actively listen, respond, improvise and get in a dialogue.

The middle ground is the semi-structured interview. It offers some benefits of the structured interview like the option of pre-interview preparation, having a general guide of the types of questions frequently asked, control over time management; and some benefits of the unstructured interview in terms of its spontaneous conversation, organically constructed natural dialogue by both the interviewer and the interviewee and a higher sense of equality of grounds between parties.

*

The second popular idea in the recruitment circles for the last few years as of 2015, is to hire for *cultural fit*. It is basically the prioritization of personality characteristics and the fit of the candidates' attitude to the organization, over the know-how or specific experience when making a hiring decision. The term was popularized by Mark Murphy in his book *Hiring for Attitude*. Organizations which can internalize this methodology are very limited but for those who can adapt this practice in their decision making, the benefits are huge. It means employees who understand the company values, principles and goals, internalizing these with a drive for a shared meaning. The top characteristics of these individuals are Coachability, Emotional Intelligence and Motivation. Seeing people only in terms of their functional expertise is a direct result of the dehumanizing gaze of industrial efficiency. When social and psychological understanding is lacking, people's performances and capabilities are considered as constants–even though they clearly fluctuate all the time in accordance with the meaning they find in their work, the flow they experience during it, and the social atmosphere and relationships they are enmeshed in. Idea of hiring for culture fit acknowledges this fact and advocates focusing more on the *fit*, rather than only focusing on the functional expertise or the know-how presented by the prospective employee. I suggest Murphy's work for anyone who is in doubt about what aspects of the candidate profile should be prioritized while making the final decision.

*

The third resource a recruiter would find, if she were making a research into materials to improve herself professionally, would be interview questions, and a whole bulk of them. To be honest, there is no shortage of interview questions. Sources like "Top [insert number here] Interview Questions" are easy to come by. They are okay places to start for those new to recruitment. They are helpful for getting an idea of which questions sit well in an interview. The problem is, extracting the information you need is not only about asking the right questions, it is about the flow of the mutual dialogue. A question that is perfect, might sound too perfect (!) or too formal when asked in an inappropriate context and risk putting distance between the interviewer and interviewee.

The other category is about interview questions that are *out of the box* or simply *weird*. Indeed, any online search regarding interview methods or techniques will find some interview question compilations that claim success against the candidates by virtue of being unexpected. Many of these questions aim to put to candidate on the spot. The main theme about them is asking questions the candidate has never heard before, therefore the idea is to observe the reasoning process of the candidate and draw conclusions on the basis of how the candidate thinks. One question asked at JetBlue for a pricing management analyst candidate was, "How many quarters would you need to reach the height of the Empire State building?" according to multiple sources such as Daily Mail, CBS News and Glassdoor (Lucas 2013). According to the same sources, Clark Construction Group's question for an office engineer candidate was "A penguin walks through that door right now wearing a sombrero. What does he say and why is he here?" A more popular one is: "Estimate how many windows are in New York," a question asked at Bain & Company to an associate consultant candidate.

*

The fourth and most important idea used by recruiters today is that of competency based interviewing. Indeed, competency based interviewing is the only theme that can be consistently defined as a *model* for interviewing. It relies on the assumption that the past behavior of a person can be used to predict future behavior.

The word *competency* is synonymous with *ability*, *capableness*, *capacity* or *faculty* according to Merriam-Webster Dictionary. In the context of human resources however, it refers to the ability of an individual to do the job properly. It is not only inclusive of cognitive skills but also behavioral skills, values and theoretical knowledge directed towards the accomplishment of the job task. Even emotional intelligence, people management skills, negotiation and stress management skills can be a part of a certain competency.

The competency based recruiting method relies on a few cornerstones. First, the job at hand is analyzed and defined in terms of the competencies needed to accomplish it. Second, these competencies create the general criteria over which the candidate is to be evaluated. Depending on the nature of the job and the direction the organization's strategy dictates, the core competencies for a certain candidate search might be; creativity, taking initiative and teamwork; while a different job might require competencies such as reliability, being service oriented, attention to detail and flexibility. The effort to define the core competencies that go with each job also helps in the creation of the competency model, that will serve as a reference point in future recruitments and performance evaluations. Third, based on the competencies defined, the candidate search and interviews commence. During the interviews, candidates' abilities to produce examples and anecdotes about their past professional experiences play the central role. These examples and anecdotes are than used as evidence or predictor of future performance.

The advantage of the method is; it limits the perceived subjectivity and therefore possible bias of the interviewer. Rather than the recruiter's completely subjective opinions about the capability of the interviewee, the past experiences discussed during the interview form the crux of the decision. STAR method is a popular framework that gives a more precise recipe on how to tell about or evaluate the set of events or experiences. It is based on understanding the Situation (which the interviewee was embedded in, the context), the Task (what needed to be done), the Action (what actually was done for the fulfillment of the task), the Result (how did it play out, success vs. failure, what is learned).

Some popular competency based questions go like this:

- *Can you give me an example of a time when you had to perform under pressure and still succeeded?*

- *Tell me about a time when you had to communicate delicate information in a sensitive way.*
- *Can you give me an example of when you had to analyze complex data and draw meaningful conclusions relevant to improving your work?*
- *Can you exemplify a situation in the past, when you have showed leadership skills amidst confusion among other team members?*

Many more examples might be included here, but you get the general idea...

There are a few disadvantages with this model as well. Most central problem is questions are easy to prepare for. Candidates can find out about what questions are asked with a very quick online search and can have all the lead time to prepare for the questions. Even if they have no knowledge of what specific questions will be asked, they can prepare and perfect a few anecdotes displaying their core competencies, and start to tell about them when triggered during the interview. Many seasoned recruiters will spot when a candidate is fixated on these triggers–they will usually repeat the question back to themselves, paraphrasing it in some minute way–as to match it with a question they already have the answer to. The other important and closely related problem is that of honesty and authenticity. Because the candidates have the lead time to prepare, the 'perfecting' of the anecdotes usually includes omission of facts that could show the interviewee in a negative light. Similarly some other anecdotes are stage to exaggerations regarding the difficulty of the situation or regarding the importance of the task, all with the common intention of creating a stronger impression.

To be clear, competency based recruiting model is not wrong. I see it as a step in the right direction. It is very helpful in defining *what* to look for while interviewing. It is also a handy mental guide to focus on and point out what the organization wants from the candidates. Not only these, but it is also a good tool for facilitating the conversation between the upper management - hiring manager - recruiter.

Though it has its benefits, it is lacking in some aspects. It functions as the shared language of what is being looked for, however it does not tell *how* to look for it–not while considering the psychology, mental state and agency of the candidate. Its language and structure of questions risk sounding unnatural, prosaic and lifeless. While questions under the competency model might technically be 'right' questions in the sense that they demand the information from the candidate clearly and directly, they do not function true to their intention when asked in a real-life dialogue. In my experience, the only candidates who are able to answer all competency questions with perfection (within the right context, concise, timely and including necessary details) are those who have practiced and rehearsed their stories enough times. The brightest profiles who have shown the best interview performance I have witnessed, have been people who told incomplete, personal, real, imperfect, complex and challenging stories. Simply put, if an anecdote is too perfect to be true, it probably isn't. We need to discover a better way.

*

The four different ideas/models I have exemplified here due to their weight in popular practice should give a solid idea about the state of scientific and theoretical knowledge surrounding recruitment and interviewing practices today. Although there are some good sources here and there, what a recruiter who is looking to be best among her colleagues can find, in terms of coherent and thought-out resources is extremely limited and repetitive.

What is Missing?

A model that goes beyond the descriptive of the basic structure of an interview is direly needed as recognized by many (Macan 2009). The *dialogue* itself is the most important aspect of the interview and as such, the science and art of it should be practiced by the professionals of this field. It is expected for the interviewers to have varying styles–this is even desired considering our stress on authenticity–but this is not to say developing the skill to conduct the crucial *interview dialogue* must be practiced by each interviewer in isolation and take decades of experience to perfect. For sure, experience is vital but theoretical understanding should feed the experience, be its bloodline. What is laid out in this book therefore, in other words, is the *theory of the dialogue*.

Experience is only valuable to the extent that it supports the learning and training of a certain skill. When theory is lacking, the effort spent becomes highly ineffective in terms of skill building. This is not unique to recruitment nor business. It is the same way in sports and arts, where skill building plays a role.

Here is the way I see the situation in recruitment today, explained through a metaphor. Given some time and some energy any individual with an average skill level and an average quality guitar can understand how the instrument works and come to produce basic tunes. Given hypothetical limitless time and energy but with no access to theoretical knowledge the guitar player might, on his own, discover how chord progressions, pentatonic scales and time signatures work and later deepen his understanding of the interplay of the melodies and rhythms. As limitless time and energy are resources we do not possess, in reality the guitar player will develop only a limited sense of music on his own, and will likely fall short of his full potential. This is where theory comes in. It can be defined as the focused and distilled totality of knowledge presented in a coherent structure that guides the experiences of the practitioner. Theory also functions as the communication framework over which different practitioners and theoreticians can discuss, further develop and improve the techniques and methods.

By studying the theory and models of learning, the newbie guitar player taps into the collective past knowledge and experience of those who played before him. Thanks to theory, mistakes can be analyzed, what needs improving is improved, what needs fixing is fixed. Most significantly, one learns from the mistakes and best practices of others in the field. Herein lies the true importance of a solid theoretical model for conducting interviews. When theory and practice are combined, they create the most valuable form of experience.

Theory without practice is dull. Experience without theory is devoid.

Long-Neglected Candidate Psychology

Any business or topic of study that ignores the qualities, characteristics and dynamics of its central subject is set to fail from the start.

If it were possible to conduct high-level chemistry without understanding the qualities, defining characteristics and states of the materials at hand, it would be possible to be good at business without understanding the customer and other stakeholders. That would mean, in recruitment, it would be possible to conduct good interviews without understanding the central stakeholder and subject-the candidate.

Does this sound absurd? It shouldn't, because the current state of the recruitment industry is a very similar reflection of this. There is either no discussion at all about the candidate psychology, or when there is, it is incredibly shallow and generic.

The governing dominant approach is centered on the job vacancy and what the organization wants, rather than what the candidate can offer. In all honesty, the recruitment process can*not* be truthfully declared as candidate-centric for a very large majority of organizations.

In many organizations, there exists this underlying and deeply rooted idea that, like in other areas of business, the desired outcome can be achieved by tackling it with aggressive decisiveness. Indeed, for the time being this seems to be an effective approach for many lines of business. More revenue can be drawn in by maximizing the marketing and sales efforts, while minimizing cost-centers and incentivizing success. The first reflex of any rapidly growing commercial organization when it confronts a target that holds potential for growth, is to directly divert its power and resources to the clear aim of either taking possession or partnering for benefit. This might be accomplished through the exploitation of the target company's natural or human resources, transfer of its key know-how that enable competition, marketing and brand positioning efforts or other merger and acquisition tactics.

Unavoidably, this business reflex shapes how organizations look at and strategize about finding and choosing talent as well. On a more strategic/macro level, organizations plan the roadmap, and then go on to assign the task of finding the executors to the recruiters and hiring managers of the organization. Ideally it should be the other way around. Talent recruitment function[*] must have a strong grip on the industry and manage its network of candidates very well, having live and up-to-date information about the allocation and limitation of human resources. It should have a feel of the 'talent market-place'

---

[*]Author's Note: Let's make the distinction between *talent* recruitment and *mass* recruitment clear. In talent recruitment, the focus is on hiring the A players and top level candidates, whereas mass recruitment is focused on recruiting large numbers of people, with not as strong competitive skill sets. When I mention the involvement of recruitment function in strategic decision making processes, I refer specifically to talent recruitment, which is involved with mid to high level, impactful hiring.

and should be an integral part of the strategic decision making process.

On the more tactical/micro level we can see how organizations tend to view the actual interview process and its stakeholders. The candidate is seen as the *passive subject* whose knowledge and qualities of character can be **extracted** through the will, bargaining power and positional strength of the organization. The candidate sits through the interview, with pleasantries and kind remarks on the surface. However the real power relation is soon made apparent through wordings, tone of voice, body language and other types of symbolic behavior (Bozionelos 2005).

If we want to develop interview techniques then we must first start with changing the way organizations perceive the candidate.

Figuratively speaking, the extraction I have mentioned is like pulling teeth. It is only possible if the candidate consents to the medical procedure and opens her mouth. All the tools, personality inventories, interview techniques and methods at the disposal of the organizations are part of its brute force and they are ineffective if the candidate a) feels threatened to be sincere or b) simply believes there is a bigger gain in "faking it". The aggressive growth-based business philosophy of the organization acts in this symbolic way, if and when it ignores the candidate psychology. Appreciating the duality of the dialogue and candidate psychology is the first step in seeing behind the mask.

The tactics of power that hold up in terms of their effectiveness in other areas of business fail in recruitment. This is precisely because in recruitment there sits a very emotional and self-reflecting individual telling a story about herself at the other end of the dialogue, rather than an organization (Murray R. Barrick 2009). Seeing behind the mask starts with appreciating the reality of the situation. I believe in the idea that, if a candidate wants to keep a certain part of her character or past in the dark, there is not much the recruiter nor the organization can do to force it out. It is therefore easier, more practical, more ethical and even more valuable to create the necessary conditions in which the candidate will willingly consent to the extraction. In other words, it cannot be *taken* by force, but only *given* voluntarily.

What I have tried to lay out here is the most fundamental issue of candidate mental state as it refers to the recruitment setting. Sharing is personal. Sharing your own story and future desires is very personal. Sharing it with someone whom you never met before feels unnatural. These are true barriers.

The Pinnacle Model acknowledges these barriers and shows ways to overcome them through its seven founding principles. The correct application of the model will enable the distance between the candidate and recruiter to be minimized, while creating the best possible conditions for the interviewer to make lasting human connections that enable an honest and thorough understanding of the interviewee. Most importantly the stage is now set for insightful observations, detailed analyses and an accurate measuring of competencies.

PART TWO: THE PRACTICE

The Pinnacle Model and the Solution Proposition

The solution is moving the interview conversation *away* from directly discussing the personality or character of the candidate herself and actually engaging in a *Naturally Flowing Conversation* on a **neutral** but related topic. Here I am referring to a conversation that is creative and interesting to both the recruiter and the candidate; is rich and fulfilling in its content; has some intellectual or technical depth; has some reference to the candidate's passions and experience or know-how; is directly or indirectly related to the role at hand.

Such a dialogue which satisfies these conditions will already include many key clues regarding the competencies, values and personality of the candidate. It is, after all a dialogue, so it will give valuable information to the candidate as well regarding the work and culture of the organization.

So you would be right to ask, how does this work?

First of all; it sets the stage for the extraction of key competencies with surgical precision: Without this form of dialogue, all questions asked by the interviewer is destined to feel **synthetic**, **unnatural**, as part of a template and most importantly lacking a unique feel to the candidate. As soon as the person interviewed feels like *just another candidate* all hope of a true dialogue is lost where the person is honest about her past, her competencies and her goals/desires.

Second; from the eyes of the candidate, the interviewer is viewed as the person who asks questions and **judges** them according to their answers. This psychology must not be ignored. Each recruiter must break this barrier in each and every interview. The simple fact that there exists a two-way conversation where the candidate has some power, gives a valuable sense of control to the other party. When both parties have some say in directing where the conversation is headed, an atmosphere of equals is ready to be reached with much more ease.

Third, conversation is a *dialogue* by definition and it is very different than an interrogation where questions are one sided. As the interview starts to sound more like the latter, the candidate will feel more and more threatened and will get more defensive. However, in a natural conversation where both parties contribute to the dialogue with comments and questions there is a much higher and *realistic* chance of honestly getting to know another person.

Fourth, asking hardcore competency based questions without achieving a naturally flowing conversation state first will trigger a defense mechanism in the candidate and the interviewer will be left with the most generic and standard of answers that sound politically correct, yes, but lack any content and fail to generate any insight.

Thus, the single most important aspect of the job interview is this: An organic, natural and spontaneously creative conversation between the candidate and interviewer. I should add that the naturally flowing conversation referred to here is different than a casual chat in both its tone and content. It has to satisfy the conditions laid out in the beginning paragraph of this chapter. It has to contain specific elements and respond to the psychology of the candidate (the needs, fears, expectations). The dialogue also needs to intersect what the job is about and the interests and competencies of the candidate. Not only that, but it has to surprise, challenge, coach, inform and more.

This approach is not incompatible with the well-established principles of competency measurement. Quite the opposite, it extends and enables it. It offers the correct frame in which it can operate and achieve results through honest answers. It is easy to ask competency based interview questions. It is harder to create the conditions for honest answers that will lead to a correct evaluation.

As mentioned before, The Pinnacle Model is a tried and true framework that has the potential to globally redefine how job interviews work. It is based on robust theory in social sciences as well as practical field experience. As a model describing the way to reach the *Naturally Flowing Conversation* in seven unique and clear principles, it can be thought as an applicable how-to guide for every recruiter and hiring manager.

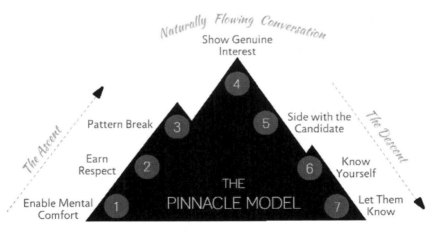

Here is the general structure and topography of the Pinnacle Model detailed: The climb up (ascent) consists of the first three principles: Enable Mental Comfort (1), Earn Respect (2), and Surprise (Pattern Break) (3). The Pinnacle is the symbolic climax of the interview and the interviewer's efforts. It is the stage both parties reach or deepen the Naturally Flowing Conversation and where the interviewer is Showing Genuine Interest (4). It also happens to be where most unconscious decisions take place. At this point, both parties have started to gain their initial impressions to build upon.

The climb down (descent) consists of the last three principles: Side with the Candidate (5), Know Yourself (6), and Let Them Know (7), after which the interview is concluded.

The ascent is more effort-intensive on behalf of the recruiter as it requires managing the mental state of the interviewee and diverting the conversation to where it needs to be. The descent is still as important and requires care (if you don't want to tumble all the way down from the top!) but can be thought as less effort-intensive once the tone and the direction of the interview has stabilized.

The Ascent - Principle 1: Enable Mental Comfort

Get the interviewee in a comfy chair. Adjust the air conditioning. Offer something to drink. Ask about the weather or traffic. Or is there more to it?

Yes there is a whole lot more to it, because we are not discussing physical comfort here, we are talking about psychological comfort and how to help the other person reach it. It is imperative for the success of the interview.

*Time pressure causes stress. It is time to slow down...*We live in a time *crushed* by the pressure to live, work, enjoy or simply experience every possible instance in the most "efficient" way. Efficiency is now an unavoidable reflex for many, specifically the white collar worker. It is like a magic ointment we apply everywhere–on every instance, without asking if it is right for the need. Everything is better when aimed at being done with maximum efficiency, right?

We talk, write, listen, communicate, work and live by efficiency. We even think of ways of relaxing in the most efficient way. We want to eat efficiently, we want to breathe efficiently. Especially in the work space, we are hardwired to think in terms of *Effort Input* versus *Value Output*. These automatic calculations never stop, and most of the time they are carried into the interview room by the interviewer and the interviewee.

Here is the problem: There are situations, which by their nature and definition, cannot be rushed or made more efficient with a mechanical approach that measures time spent versus information gathered. In these cases a precisely defined structure, intentions for better optimization, calculating for fewer actions or simply installing more order, planning, regulation and logicality aren't helpful. Take the process of meeting someone for instance. The act of "getting to know" someone relies on a **natural** and **unforced** interaction between two or more people. If and when there is time pressure, the interaction becomes limited, forced and unnatural by definition... Getting to know someone in their habitus–their natural way of acting that defines their personality structure–becomes impossible.

The need for time management is very real in a world of constantly changing priorities. It is in many cases desirable. As such, our fetish for efficiency is likely to survive for the foreseeable future. My point here is this; like there are domains in the day of the average professional that do benefit from time management and efficiency orientation; there are other domains that *do not* benefit from rushing it. Some situations receive more harm than good when the reigning priority is efficiency and the biggest pressure is that of time management. Issues where this stress is most felt tend to focus around people related lines of business. We might be able to cut down the time needed to prepare a daily operations report in MS Excel from 50 minutes to 10 minutes with good practice and some short-cuts; we can't cut down the time to *get to know someone* if we are talking about a genuine interaction.

So, slow down.

It is indeed strikingly simple. As the interviewer, you have to slow down and relax. Think of the interview as if it is in a time bubble. No distraction or pressure allowed from the outside. Think of it as a kind of meditation if it makes it easier to practice. However, at all costs, you have to lead the way for the mental state of the interviewee. If the recruiter is tense, in a rush, upset or impatient, it is unlikely the candidate will be in a relaxed and comfortable mood.

When the interview starts, all other responsibilities should come to a halt. There are no e-mails, there are no calls, there are no "next meetings". No worry about work, children, money and traffic. In this sense the job of the interviewer can be thought similar to that of a therapist. Regardless of the day the therapist is having, when a client session is on, the therapist has to be in a positive or neutral mode and lead the way for the open and relaxed dialogue. As the recruiter, you need to be there, in the room, with the candidate *a hundred percent*. When the interview starts there is only the world of the candidate, and the world of the interviewer.

Fear and comfort don't co-exist. Fear is triggered by potential threats. Discover what is perceived as a threat from the candidate point of view and openly address them. A good recruiter asks good questions but the best ones see the situation as a whole. Look at all the pieces of puzzle. Why is the person in front of you? What is the motivation? What is she afraid of? Let's be honest here, it is a job interview. The person across you is not there because she likes you, or is your friend. There is a very specific mindset and agenda: To get the job (even if it involves being semi-honest on some issues). The candidate most likely has concerns about feeling inferior, being judged or criticized harshly for her decisions, being made to feel inadequate. She might hold anxiety about being in a situation in which she thinks she has to lie. She might have resurfacing guilt about past failures, career success and self-worth... Any or all of the above are very natural and standard parts of the candidate psychology. According to the social and economic status, age, occupation and expectation of the candidate, these will vary. The recruiter or the hiring manager needs to use intuition and improvise if necessary to get a feel for what the candidate is worried about.

So what to do in practice? The interviewer, if she wishes to comfort the candidate, needs to know and understand these general threat areas very well. On top of this, a great deal of effort should be put in intuitively understanding candidate-specific threat areas. The introduction (and the opening dialogue) should acknowledge that the job interview is not our most natural states; should openly show respect, but be warm rather than diplomatic. It should state the intention of the interview process and the intentions of the interviewer, while mentioning that the real purpose is not the judge, but to get to know a real person. Critically, it should emphasize that the more honest and true to her self the candidate can be, the interview, too can be a better experience for both parties.

A few emphatic words, an emphasis on honesty, a single statement showing you are going to stay away from being judgmental opens all the doors. *Just simply tell the candidate this is an interview based on honesty and openness.* Clearly tell what you are looking for above all is cooperation in establishing a genuine and authentic dialogue. You would be shocked how much of an effect this makes in many of the cases. It is as if some people have been waiting for this cue for all their life, and the structure of the interview changes dramatically for the better after this point on. The candidate is already in a need to act this way. Some simple words, but includes a very powerful message that resonates in the mind of the candidate for the duration of the interview. It should be needless to say, the interviewer should respond in kind when it comes to honesty and openness and not act in any manner that can be interpreted as an open or disguised threat including gaze, tone of voice, unexpected reactions etc.

Show sincerity and warmth. The world is changing. The tough, pushy, constantly challenging, diplomatic and self-centered interviewer model does not work anymore because it ignores the candidate psychology. Sure, there needs to be some structure and a high level of mutual respect, but beyond this try to be less diplomatic and more on the side of the candidate.

Warmth is easy to get. It is a familiar feeling (hopefully) for most of us, one that we experience near people we care about or who care about us. Unless we have a reason for negative emotions towards the candidate, nothing is gained by not showing some basic/minimum level of warmth upon first contact.

Sincerity is harder to master, especially when there are high levels of time pressure and never ending back-to-back interviews. Sincerity, obviously by definition, can't be faked. It can only be achieved through honesty. In my experience, feeling appreciation for the chance to get to know another person, and enjoying the experience of broadening your world vision vicariously through someone else's eyes, is the best source of motivation and coincidentally, of sincerity. In other words, when there is curiosity, there is sincerity.

Another suggestion is to *match* the candidate's level of intimacy. Some people are more introverted, in such cases; you should take a step back in tone and content and have a conversation in more contemplative way, leaving a wider area for hard-hot topics. Some candidates are more extroverted and start acting open and intimate more quickly. Again, try to match this with tone and content, dig in and respond in kind with more questions. When an introvert has to act in an extroverted kind of way, this puts tension on the psyche and the natural dialogue starts to suffer. So try to create the atmosphere in which the candidate can express herself in her most neutral state. Introversion and extroversion (although they are very central traits in character) are only one example to many dimensions. Matching the candidate's level in other areas such as thought and speech tempo can be thought as part of a coupled dance. When you are in harmony; a real dialogue where the candidate *creates* her story is possible, at other times you will be hearing a mental script that may or may not be truthful.

These key ideas are a good starting pointing for comforting the candidate psychologically and setting the stage for the rest of the interview.

Let me share a personal note before moving on. As I wrote down these principles which I had discovered and have been practicing to the best of my abilities, I realized more and more that putting these into action is more about *being* than doing. Many of the tips here will make sense when analyzed individually and hopefully can find some space in your own practices. However, for a complete/holistic integration of all these principles into practice and becoming the best interviewer you can be, you will probably have to revisit some very fundamental personal values and ideas about the human nature you yourself hold. Curiosity, regard for other individuals' stories, our fragility against anxiety, respect and transparency are some of these core values, the rest will make themselves apparent as we proceed.

Key Takeaways

- Time pressure causes stress. The interview is a time to slow down, relax and take your time.

- A relaxed candidate will be more honest; the mental and emotional mood of the interview should be led by the interviewer.

- Fear and comfort can't co-exist. Fear is triggered by potential threats. Discover what is perceived as a threat from the candidate's perspective and openly address them.

- Show sincerity and warmth.

- Match the candidate in trait, tone and tempo of thought and speech to the best of your abilities.

The Ascent - Principle 2: Earn Respect

The second principle of the Pinnacle Model is to *Earn Respect*.

Respect, like trust, must be *earned*.

Do not be fooled in thinking each new candidate that comes through the door respects you, the recruiter/interviewer/hiring manager, by default. How can they be truly respecting you if they have not met you before? With a good degree of confidence we can say this: It is your company, position, title and decision making capacity that they respect–not your person.

If you are after the honest and genuine dialogue we have mentioned, you have got to earn the candidate's respect. I dare say, you have to fight for it with everything you got. Because like comforting the candidate, this is imperative for a real dialogue that will result in understanding the world from the candidate's perspective in addition to learning about her knowledge level and job history.

The candidate has to respect you as a human being, as a person independent of your job title. She should say to herself as the interview intensifies: "This is someone who knows what he is talking about. This is someone who has the capacity to understand me."

This is a crucial point. Without exception, in every interview, every candidate (consciously or unconsciously) asks herself the question: "Is this person sitting in front of me capable of understanding me?" The answer to this question marks a turning point. It defines the content, depth and quality of the rest of the interview and each answer to the questions asked then on. If the answer is a "no", or a "maybe"; you might as well stop the interview right then and there and hand a questionnaire instead. Because the answers you get will be regurgitated, cliché, textbook answers that won't help with truly getting to know the person of interest.

So in essence, when the candidate asks herself "Is this person capable of understanding my line of business, my professional and individual life choices?" the answer must be a definite "yes". This answer can only be yes, if there is enough respect from the candidate towards the recruiter.

As the level of respect increases, so does the level of trust. From the candidate's perspective it is the trust that she will not spend a good deal of time and energy trying to communicate something that will not be understood, or worse misunderstood.

Okay, earning the respect of the candidate in each and every interview seems important. But how do we earn this respect?

Earn respect with knowledge first, attitude later. I have discovered when we are talking about respect, lots of people tend to start thinking about looking powerful, confident, acting and talking with a sharp decisiveness and conviction. While these are good to have, focusing only on them would be to miss the point. The essence of the issue is about showing that you are capable, knowledgeable, interested and visionary. The attitude will help, but bear in mind it is complimentary, not the essence. The trick is displaying, or rather *hinting at* your level of knowledge without being braggy about it. Think of the cumulative knowledge you hold as an iceberg; let the peak be visible and leave the rest for the imagination. In many instances, telling the right amount of knowledge is better than smothering the person with everything you know about the topic.

This is indeed a fine balance, although with variance from culture to culture, showing off has a consistently negative undertone, whereas humility seems to be a unifying positive trait. Since we are trying to earn respect, coming of as snob would defeat the purpose. While holding your composure and humility, look for openings to engage in discussions that require both parties to be knowledgeable.

Show you have a very strong grasp of the candidate's field of expertise. Imagine you are recruiting for a User Experience (UX) Specialist position. You have to go well beyond the job description written out and converse fluently in the language of the candidate. You have to be able to speak 'User Experience'. You have to be able to speak to the candidate with the same depth as if you were colleagues in the same department. Your conversation should include topics like: How has the field of UX expertise emerged in the last decade? How are 'design thinking' and 'customer journey' parts of creating a user experience? How are UX teams challenged by the other teams in the organization? Who are the opinion leaders in this area?

Being able to speak the same language with the candidate determines the level of knowledge and competency you can extract in the dialogue. When and if what the candidate is saying starts to sound foreign to you, it would be wishful thinking to assume you can adequately judge her level and ability to do the job. Having a strong grasp of the specific field is not optional, rather it is a prerequisite for being a good recruiter. It is also an integral part of earning respect.

Go deep. Prove yourself as someone who can discuss specifics, who has technical and/or intellectual depth. Don't hesitate to bring out really specific topics that are thought to be only known by people who have become experts in their area. If we stick with the UX example, talk about the vices and virtues of the X or Y Guided User Interface (GUI) platform. Or go further and challenge the candidate about her stand on minimalism and what flat design has to do with it? At this point a naturally flowing dialogue should be emerging and taking root. Also refer to what is *hot*. It will show your interest in the field is not at a textbook level but a real part of your personality. As I have mentioned before, this is the part where it starts to be more about *being* than doing. It is acceptable to display a shallow level of knowledge on a topic, yet it is a challenge to show nuanced and in-depth knowledge if you are not personally interested in the area you are recruiting for. Let's say, if you are recruiting for a digital marketing role, talk about the trend for online-offline integration and how the landscape will be in the near and far future when it comes to pricing marketing campaigns. Talk about the changing collective nature of the internet, the motivation behind crowdfunded campaigns, the use of browser advertisement blockers and challenges about privacy that comes with more quantifiable information about each person. It should be given that in addition to personal interest, there needs to be some serious background work here prior to the interview as well. Nobody said it was easy!

Look towards the future. Share what you know with openness and ask for the candidate to cooperate in the same way, together share a vision, imagine a world, try to understand and speculate about the future. Sticking with the digital marketing theme, try to discuss how Augmented and Virtual Reality will shape new marketing campaigns to come or how online spending habits will be in five to ten years. (A tip: Usually, the best and brightest people in a given line of business will have a lot to say and contribute when discussing the future. They will also enjoy this conversation more, in contrast to the average people who tend to stick more with common and safe answers.) Crafting an idea about the future brings the recruiter and the candidate closer and to a certain point that makes the candidate say to herself, "… this is not bad, this guy has vision, his only concern isn't filing the job opening ASAP, but he cares about this role and industry." This idea will bury itself deep in the mind of candidate. It will also likely be accompanied by a feeling of self-congratulation and pride due to the importance given to the candidate's field of expertise.

Show tenure, seniority, composure and integrity. Attitude may not be the core message here; but it is still very important to some people. This is especially important when interviewing people with significantly longer experience and tenure in the field. Display and if necessary exemplify that you are confident and respected in your field, you can even give credit to some major and critical projects you have accomplished to earn the respect of the candidate. Even if you are not the most senior person in the room, you can make up for this with composure, curiosity and the competence you display.

Key Takeaways

- Fight for the respect of the candidate. Do not take it for granted.
- Show you have a very strong grasp of the candidate's field of expertise.
- Keep humility in check, but prove yourself as someone who can discuss specifics, who has technical or intellectual depth.

- Talk about what's hot, share a vision, inspire and impress the candidate.

The Ascent - Principle 3: Surprise (or Pattern Break)

Third principle of *The Pinnacle Model* is to **Surprise** or what I also like to call **Pattern Break**.

Let's start with a fact. An overwhelming majority of our actions are dictated by what can be defined as simple **habits**. A habit may simply be described as a way of doing a mundane task, without exhausting too much cognitive resource. This is a crude but fair explanation. A habit can also be described as the path most travelled. It might not be the fastest, the most efficient or the easiest route, but it *feels* as if it is the most convenient simply due to the fact that it has been repeated a good number of times. For the route most travelled; risks, reactions and outcomes are well known and prepared for. So in essence what we call habits are shortcuts that save us the trouble of calculating the pros and cons of each new situation over and over again. A world without habits isn't realistic or possible; and if it were, it would most likely be intolerable. The simple daily life events of an urbanite requires a huge number of micro-decisions, if we were to stop and think, in other words use concentrated cognitive resource, for each of them we would be exhausted.

Habits however, contrary to some people might think, are not only about actions or daily routines of behavior. In other words, they are not only about doing but also about ideas and ways of thinking. True to its origins, the word *Habitual Thinking* does a good job of summarizing this. If we are in a situation we have faced before, the first reflex is to refer back to our experience and imagine a mental model of what we have felt, thought and interpreted. These ideas, then go on to form the basis for the second experience and on and on goes this cycle. This is the main reason first meetings, first impressions and other *firsts* are considered so important. It is also the reason why misconceptions are difficult to overcome. Put clearly, we do not use patterns and habits only for decisions in physical-material reality, but also for abstract thoughts, mental actions and specifically while decoding a conversation and responding to it.

What do these patterns or habits have to do with the interview? This is a fair question and deserves to be answered very clearly. These habits are an important part of the interviewer-interviewee dialogue. It is not only the recruiters or the hiring managers who have made a habit of asking their go-to questions. The candidates also do this in their own way. Drawing on their past experiences, there are questions that they expect to hear. The answers to these questions are also well practiced and polished. The problem with habitual thinking patterns manifests itself most clearly when a candidate mistakes the specific question you have asked for a generic and frequently asked interview question; and starts answering accordingly, or with an answer lacking a direct response.

Consider this. You are asking the interviewee a question about what makes the most successful people achieve their position, in other words, what makes them who they are. What might the answer be? You might think the answer may vary in the domains of the factors that create success, such as the character traits of the person, the education and family background advantages, their sense of risk, luck, a nose for sensing newer trends?... However, a candidate accustomed to hearing the more frequently asked question *"What are your strengths and weaknesses?"* will show the tendency towards answering this, rather than the original question. The answer is determined more so by what the listener is thinking, than the question itself. We can confidently say that the preconceptions and expectations of both parties–as well as their thinking habits play a big role in determining the dialogue.

Not all candidates experience this to the same degree. For the sake of simplicity let's say there are two kinds of candidates. The first group is those with very little to none interviewing experience. The second group is that of senior professionals who have had at least ten interviews in their careers. The first group is already in an advantage, as their lack of experience also means they are more open (in terms of not knowing what to expect) and do not think only within established cycles of habitual thoughts and reflexes. They can be thought more in terms of a *Tabula Rasa,* blank slate. In this group, a naturally flowing conversation where parties can get to know each other is easier to establish.

Senior professionals of the second group however, have already started to carve out their own reflexes when it comes to a job interview. They have their own ideas (positive and negative) associated with the prospect of recruitment, the interview processes, recruiters themselves and hiring managers. More importantly, they have had a few successful and a few unsuccessful dialogues in the past. And now, are more suave about how they represent themselves and more shrewd on what to say/what to hold back. They also tend to experience selective hearing more, or show tendency to divert the conversation away from the questions and into their perfected story. In other words, they have developed some strong patterns of habitual thinking.

What do we do with a pattern? Break it.

What the interviewer must accomplish is to surprise and break thinking patterns candidate walks in with. The message you as the interviewer should give is clear: "This is not an ordinary interview." Your words and actions should speak loudly and communicate the message that trite, conventional, copied, worn-out, stereotypical answers will not do. The candidate's assumptions about the type of recruiter or hiring manager you are and the type of interview this is about to be, should be broken.

The candidate must be, in a manner of speaking, surprised or faced with the unexpected.

During the interview, candidate should be facing a situation that is at least slightly different than the expectation. This is the key to starting a genuine dialogue. Consider the opposite, in a dialogue when the candidate leaves the interview thinking it was same with or very similar to all the other interviews she had, would you think she had experienced an authentic and revealing dialogue? As the interview itself becomes unique, the candidate will show a more unique side of her; as the interview becomes monotonous and conventional, the candidate will show a more conventional, ordinary side of her as well.

Surprise through engaging in creativity. Talking about ourselves is a creative storytelling process. The content might not be different but each time your story is told it is recreated, if it is genuine one. As Bergström and Knights conclude in their research: *"Any attempt to analyse the impact of organizational discourse on individual subjectivity must take into account the possibility that subjects actively take part in their own self-construction and that this construction is produced in social interaction"* (Ola Bergström, David Knights 2006). The self-construction here refers to the *story* of the candidate that is created in relation to the live dialogue happening with the recruiter. This finding makes the interview even more important and crucial for the evaluation of the candidate. If the content is memorized and not created through the social interaction, it will sound stale and lacking in detail. The best and quickest way of engaging the creative instinct is to challenge the candidate to tell their story from another perspective. A question that exemplifies this could go like this: "...on the topic of design, based on your experiences I see *design thinking* is important to you. Let's imagine for a moment; if you had looked at optimizing the leisure time you have and what you personally want to accomplish in life as a design problem, how would you approach it?" This kind of an approach forces the hand of the interviewee to improvise on a matter they know well. It not only shows their competence on approaching a known topic from a fresh perspective, it also gives insight about aspects of personality otherwise obscured from view of the interviewer.

Surprise with the structure of the interview. Break the chronological pattern. A typical interview starts with introductory pleasantries followed up with the cue, "Please tell about yourself/your CV" and after letting the candidate speak for a while, the interviewer will ask questions such as "Why did you apply for this job?" or "Why do you want this role and what can you bring to it?" and will go on with further similar questions in the lines of "How do you like to be managed?", "Why did you leave your last job?", "Are you a team-player?" etc... Instead of sticking to this structure, try mixing it up.

A good example might start with asking about the previous interviews the candidate has been to or by asking if they enjoy interviewing for jobs, following up with why or why not. A better example might involve delaying talking about the job for a few moments and instead (with minimum time pressure) talking about a topic the candidate is passionate about other than work. Another example I have found to be effective is after welcoming the candidate, sharing your opinion on a specific matter and asking if the candidate agrees on it or not, and then moving on the dialogue from there. Basically all of these will serve the same purpose. When the interviewee finds herself in a dialogue with an unfamiliar structure, the reflex will be to rely more on spontaneous creation of answers rather than telling fixed responses to expected questions. The idea that it is not 'just another interview' will be emboldened.

Surprise by probing with questions that are not necessarily expected in the context of a standard interview. This item is deeply conjoined with the previous item as questions are the number one tool for diverting the flow of the interview.

Whereas the previous idea is about the chronology of the questions and the topography of the interview, this is more about the actual content and type of the questions. What you as the interviewer want to question might not dramatically change from one candidate to the other, but there are practically unlimited ways to approach questioning a certain competency. Think of it both ways, if you were the candidate, how honestly, creatively and authentically could you answer a question that had been asked you for the seventh time? Keeping on with the theme 'this is not just another interview', try asking questions that are out of the box, but still take a relevant jab at what you want to measure. To clarify, we are broadly talking about any question (while in the limits of ethics and respect) that a candidate has not prepared for. An example might go like this: "What did you think when Yanis Varoufakis, Valve's Former Steam Market Economist, became Greece's finance minister?", "How do you see the future of VR (Virtual Reality) headsets now that HTC is in the competition with HTC Vive?" or "Do you think Elon Musk's vision of colonizing Mars is realistic, how does this effect the technologies we have today and will have in the coming years?"

Finally, surprise with the way you position yourself in the interview and with the way you approach the candidate. In other words, try to mix your routine, and **take on different hats.** Do not always be the recruiter who asks recruiting questions, but also be the businessman who asks about financial stability of the company, be the geek who is really curious about Onion Architecture, be the tourist who is looking for advice on a place the candidate has recently visited, be the biker, be the intellectual, be the psychologist, be the career advisor, be the pessimist, be the dreamer. Each hat you take on should reflect a unique identity, your tone, approach and the content of your comments and questions should be focused, even if for a moment, on the aim of making the candidate forget this is a job interview.

To sum up, the key ideas here are variety and curiosity. As long as you remain loyal to these two and help the candidate live through a different, unique interview; the chances of truly getting to know another person's character, desires and passions increase greatly.

Key Takeaways

- Understand how habits work in the structuring of mental models and consequently in interview dialogues.
- Understand how repetition and routine may work against the authenticity sought after in an interview.
- Break thinking patterns and habits through the use of wit, creativity and curiosity.
- Use your ability to structure the interview and determine the content of the questions to your advantage and surprise the

candidate. Change the routine with the way you open up the dialogue, with the questions you ask, with the way you address. Let the candidate know this isn't just another interview, where she can get away with pouring out memorized answers.

The Pinnacle - Principle 4: Show Genuine Interest

Showing genuine interest and displaying this vividly to the interviewee is the fourth principle of the Pinnacle Model. After the first three principles of ascent, this principle discusses the experience of *being* at the top. As made clear, showing genuine interest is the focus here. By definition *genuineness* relies on being truly curious about the content of the candidate's story and the structure of the candidate's character. It is also about enjoying the moment of the conversation, and on a broader level the occupation of recruitment itself.

If you are in an industry of people operations or human resources, you must have heard popular phrases like *discover your passion* or *do what you love and you don't have to work for a day in your life*. Now to be honest, I don't know if this is possible in the working conditions of 2015 and for most of the world... So I would like to advise some healthy skepticism against those who relentlessly advocate similar ideas.

Each career pursuit has some highs and lows in it. What is **constant** is that there needs to be an essential motivating factor for each of us. This might be (and is for most people) power & wealth; desire for leadership, altruism & desire to do good, self-fulfillment, career advancement, future stability and so on. The main motivating factor may vary, and that's perfectly fine. The point is discovering this motivation gives important clues about the structure of character and the values you put weight in as a person.

On a personal note; this for me is learning and curiosity. I see myself as a very curious person by nature who likes finding things out and learning new skills–I do not discriminate topics when it comes to learning. Discovering about a neutron star or a new way to engage mass attention on an online media platform is very pleasurable to me. Considering my time in quite a few different sectors and recruiting for almost hundreds of different types of roles, I can say this with confidence: *Recruiting is one of the best careers for inherently curios people.*

All the polymaths and renaissance men of the world, hear me out! If you are motivated by learning about new things, new people, new topics, new perspectives; or see a great value in sharing the wisdom of senior professionals and engaging in challenging yet constructive dialogues with them, I can't think of a better fit for a career choice than recruitment. On the other hand, if inherent motivation by genuine curiosity is not your thing, don't be a recruiter. For people motivated by other factors than curiosity, a career in recruitment might feel repetitive and be short-lived. If you are not excited about the prospect of seeing life from the eyes of others, if you are pessimistic about what you can learn from other people, there is very little chance you can be a really good recruiter/interviewer or get really good at your role as a hiring manager.

Quite a few things happen when you, as the recruiter or hiring manager accomplish being genuinely curious about the candidate and show the interest during an interview.

The first is; you and the candidate are saved from mutual boredom. This may not seem much of a benefit at first, but it is actually rather important. No constructive dialogue was achieved through apathy. *When you show genuine interest, you and the candidate remain engaged, on topic and alive.* You do not slide into that unavoidable routine of asking the same boring questions only to hear the same answer from candidates as bored as you are. The more curios you are by nature, the longer it will take you to slide into a feeling of routine. During the interview you are engaging with a professional who is diverting a huge part of her concentration to understanding you. Naturally, the moment you begin losing interest, most smart candidates will pick up on this. Rather than faking being interested in what the interviewee is saying and repeating a mechanical nodding action–showing true interest will take the conversation to a new level. To be fair, this is not always possible. Not what all the interviewees say all the time will be interesting. My point is this; the more curious by nature you are, it is easier to find something of interest during the dialogue and thus remain highly engaged a bigger percent of the time. What peaks your interest might not necessarily be the content of what you hear. The body language, the emotion attached with a recently used phrase, a microexpression, or a value judgment about a topic or a person might be among many of the details which can be extracted even from the most mundane of conversations. Take microexpressions for example. Microexpressions are involuntary, uncontrollable, and universally constant facial expressions that typically last under half a second. They correspond with major emotions such as disgust, anger, fear, sadness, happiness, surprise and contempt. Observing these and having curiosity about discovering the emotional state of the candidate (and calibrating your response with the intention of creating a positive environment) is in itself a whole category of discovery enough to curb curiosity.

Put other way, the curiosity of mention here is not necessarily always about what the candidate is saying–the content; but also in many instances about who the candidate is–the total personality waiting to be discovered.

The second major point is about enjoyment. We could even call this being in the *state of play*. It is the point when you stop worrying about where you are, how you represent yourself and what you ultimately want to accomplish but focus on the flow of the dialogue itself and enjoy the beauty of sharing a perspective, sharing a way of looking at the world around you with another individual. When you are truly interested in the person or in the topics you are discussing, this mutual understanding takes root much faster. With that, content of the conversation and the quality of both the questions and the answers increase exponentially. You multiply the chance of engaging in a naturally flowing conversation, the pinnacle point for the successful interview where you honestly get to know another person, and come to enjoy working as a recruiter. Believe this; that feeling of enjoyment is contagious, as it *will* be picked up by the candidate. I honestly hope the recruitment process, and the moment of the interview will evolve to be seen as huge opportunities for learning and self-discovery on behalf of the candidates, and a part of continuous learning for the recruiters and hiring managers, rather than inauthentic, bureaucratic, stressful obstacles.

The third point is about *shifting perspective*: The ability to see the world from the point of view of another person. This is in line with the idea of not only being interested in the content of what the interviewee says but actually the total world view and qualities of the perspective of the person across you. Here it is important to be as transparent as possible and clearly display you have come to understand and share their perspective. This can be accomplished by showing appreciation for some idea, someone or something the interviewee likes or values. Alternatively, this can also be achieved by critiquing an interesting or engaging topic that is of concern to the candidate. These all work towards the ultimate aim of making the other person feel understood, which can in turn be used to first build a meaningful connection and late to build a unique relationship. During the interview, it is about taking an emotional perspective. As Brian Miller says in his inspiring talk about the role of changing perspective in magic (Miller 2015), sometimes the easiest way of determining the emotional perspective is to first ask and then later concentrate all the effort to actually listening the person, rather than spending the cognitive effort to formulating our next question or response, as we are guilty of doing some of the time. I completely buy into this idea, at times, concentrating more on which question to ask rather than listening to what the candidate is saying is a vice even the best of us are guilty of. We can all benefit from practicing active listening more.

As a final point relating to genuine interest, I would like to suggest a trick. The key to keeping curiosity sharp at all times is constantly coming up with new hypotheses. This is inherently about what I call *theorizing*. Each tentative or certain decision or judgment you make about a certain quality of the interviewee should go through a process of theorizing, testing and comparing before the conclusion. Candidate valuation by itself can't be categorized as scientific, due to its subjective and personal nature. However there is always room for improvement. Theorizing gives recruiters and hiring managers the option to calibrate their own evaluations and biases for internal consistency between candidates. It also helps with more realistic and robust evaluations. The Halo Effect, named by the psychologist Edward Thorndike, suggests we are prone to the cognitive bias in which the observer's overall impression of a person influences ideas and feelings about the person's character or qualities. In other terms, we are more likely to group positive observations with positive ones and negative observations with negative ones. Let's interpret: This means, if we were to make a representative chart showing the weight of positive and negative qualities a candidate displays during the interview and could plot the negative qualities on the left, neutral qualities in the middle and the positive qualities on the right, our graphs would be skewed to either one side or the other, leaving the middle of the graph relatively empty. Candidates who have very strong attributes in the positive side would be judged under a more positive light for their other qualities. Vice versa, candidates who display a few very strongly negative attributes would have a tough time pointing out their positive qualities. Theorizing is beneficial for resisting against the Halo Effect.

If this flow of hypotheses generation is not happening before you make decisions about an aspect/quality of the candidate, your conclusions are more likely to be based on gut feelings, superstitions and prejudices. Moreover, it might point out to the dangerous tendency of grouping normally independent qualities with each other and result in skewed judgments. Although our gut feeling tells us the opposite, someone well might be assertive, competitive and impulsive on one hand, and warm, open to change and resourceful on the other. These are all independent aspects of a person's character as laid out clearly in the personality factors model (Raymond Catell, Herbert W. Bernard, Maurice M. Tatsuoka 1970). Awareness of our own limitations and biases in judgment is another topic in its own, and we will discover it in the following sections.

We can firmly conclude, this is more about *being* than *doing* (following practical tips). The vision of this principle is hard to recreate by following simple steps which the practitioner has not internalized. It is more closely associated with the character of the recruiter or hiring manager. Success depends on whether the character of the interviewer (in terms of curiosity) is a good fit for the job of extracting information from the interviewee. If the idea we believe is that humans can only be understood through emphatic human connection, it should follow that the genuineness of the interviewer must be a precondition for eliciting genuine reactions from the interviewee–which is what we desire in the first place.

Key Takeaways

- Recruiting is one of the best careers for inherently curios people; if you are not a curious person, there is little chance you can be a great recruiter.
- In an interview, always be curious; not always about what the candidate is saying–the content, but also in many

instances about who the candidate is–their personality.

- Make sure to have fun and enjoy the conversation.
- Shift perspective, make the interviewee feel understood.
- Theorize.
- Mind the cognitive traps.

The Descent - Principle 5: Side with the Candidate

This is about setting your priorities straight. *Be a consultant first, side with the candidate and you will create connections that are deeper, last longer and give you better insight.*

I should make clear what is exactly meant by 'siding with the candidate.' First of all, it means prioritizing getting to know the person over filling the job vacancy. There are very real pressures as we will discuss very shortly, and as such, getting to know the candidate might not be the number one business priority outside the duration of the interview, this is natural in the business world today. But *during* the interview itself, there exists only the dialogue with the candidate. The number one priority is getting to know the person. Looking at the recruitment process in a candidate-centric way, rather than a job-vacancy-centric way means the competencies and capabilities of the candidate are evaluated holistically, not only in terms of the competencies that are defined in the recruitment brief. Second, it means asking the question "Which job in the organization would be a best fit for John?" more often than "Which candidates we have interviewed fit the job criteria?" Third and most importantly, it means clearly communicating the message that you as the recruiter or the hiring manager are there to help, be a consultant, be a guide in a world of highly complicated career choices. See the candidate as an ally. Although a recruiter or a hiring manager might have the duty to evaluate and prioritize stronger candidates, they can and should use their positional knowledge in an effort to guide the thinking patterns and future choices of the candidate in a positive manner.

What separates the good from the great, when it comes to recruiting is the ability to side with the candidate, *despite* all the barriers and limitations.

Recruitment is not an easy job. Many recruiters have their own Key Performance Indicators (KPIs) that are used in measuring their efficacy and success rate. Among these, time to fill an opening, the number of interviewed candidates, the number of long and short listed candidates are common. So there is a very real time pressure that is hard to manage. Even in settings which lack formal KPIs, the real life business demands remain. The similar pressures of time to fill a position, prepare a longlist of pre-screened candidates to the agreed contract standards or Service-Level Agreements (SLAs) are constant. It is not at all uncommon for a recruiter to manage more than 10 to 30 different projects, all of which have their own job requirements and own candidate lists/pools, simultaneously. For hiring managers, there is different set of difficulties. In many organizations, the work load is traditionally optimized with regards to normal operational capacity of the team. When one or more of the team members leave the team, this in itself creates an extra workload for the remaining team members and the team manager. So even before the hiring manager is involved in the recruiting process she already has her hands full and in need of a resource as soon as possible. The case is quite similar when the growing of the business rather than an employee replacement triggers the process. More often than not, many teams will be at or past their working capacity before the final decision for a new recruitment is made.

Due to these dynamics, the recruitment process characteristically starts off with a sense of urgency and time pressure driven by real business needs. As a way to manage this time pressure, the first common tactics are to cut the time for candidate research and sourcing (leading to a decline in the quality of the candidates); and to increase the number of interviews (leading to a heavier work load and less resource to approach the recruitment process strategically). In more concise terms, if and when there is backbreaking time pressure, quantity is prioritized over quality. The cumulative effect of these factors for most recruiters and hiring managers is, heavy operational work load, which in turn causes a bigger and tougher problem: *Alienation*.

A Tough Problem: Alienation from Candidates

As the business and performance pressure the recruiter or hiring manager has to shoulder increases, the capacity to empathize with the candidate decreases. Expectedly, the business priority of many commercial institutions that specialize in recruiting is, measurable profitability. As a direct result of this, many processes are quantity based rather than quality. This is simply due to the fact that quality is hard to measure when people are the main variable in the equation. Quantity based metrics on the other hand are easily measurable and displayable. The unfortunate part is that, although the quality of the interview (thus choosing the right fits for the job) has a very strong and direct effect when it comes to business, this is still very hard to measure.

Understandably, when a recruiter has to manage seven back-to-back interviews in a single day, she becomes more a machine than human and becomes alienated to her surroundings and working conditions. Acting as a consultant who sides with the candidate and engages in a real authentic dialogue becomes a real tough task under these circumstances.

Let us take a step back and see what alienation is from a wider perspective. Alienation is not a recruitment specific, or even an industry specific problem. It is, on the contrary, a general problem that is shared through sectors, industries and different lines of business. It is a complex social issue and what I can do here is only recommend a more in-depth reading of the concepts of *social alienation* and *economic alienation*.

For the sake of furthering our argument let's go with the simplest definition. It is defined by

Robert Ankony as *"a condition in social relationships reflected by a low degree of integration or common values and **a high degree of distance or isolation** between individuals."* Alienation can also be defined as the increased distance from the end effect of the action taken towards creating the desired effect. When a rural farmer plows the field, the effect it creates is very direct and obvious, the aeration of the field. The plowing, the seeding, the watering and the tending of the field create the desired end result–a better harvest. The harvest and its results are easily observed and experienced by he who plows, seeds, waters and tends the field. In an inverse situation where an imaginary 'industrial farmer' only works in the operation of the machine which creates the right size of plastic bags used in the packaging of the seeds to be distributed to farmlands, he can be said to be more alienated from others who work towards same desired end result and from the end value creation itself–the harvest.

The dangers of alienation should be a recruiter's concern because it determines whether she can see the candidates as human beings at the end of a long day, rather than printed piles of CV's or numbers on a long list. Alienation is characterized by isolation between the individuals and a disability to find common denominators. It should be perfectly clear that this is the **exact opposite** of how a candidate - recruiter dialogue should be. It is a great barrier that is created by the way our economic relations are structured and heightened by the delivery pressures of the job and its repetitive operational tasks. More operational workload (in this case conducting a big quantity of back-to-back interviews) causes more alienation and distancing from the subject of the interview, the candidate.

Defining these limitations is valuable, not because they give us valid excuses, but because defining and understanding them should help us in overcoming them. So let us ask the question,

"What sets apart a great recruiter from a good one?" My answer would go like this: A good recruiter can connect and establish a naturally flowing conversation in some circumstances and with some candidates (incidentally and by gut feeling); a great recruiter however can do this consistently and systematically. A great recruiter can side with the candidate even when up against the barriers and limitations we have defined here such as time pressure, business demands, unreasonable candidates, stress and risks of alienation.

What else sets apart a great recruiter?

- A great recruiter finds the self-motivation to concentrate fully on the interview itself, being in the room with the candidate a hundred percent.

- A great recruiter is passionate about learning, has a high level of curiosity about business and people, and uses this driving motivating force in overcoming alienation.

- A great recruiter understands what lies at the core of the job very well: It is not shortlists, longlists, business briefs, candidate reports, and definitely not the number of candidates reviewed. It is, before anything else, the dialogue with the candidate, the climax of which is the interview.

All great recruiters understand they are on the same team with the candidate, they wholeheartedly see where the value is created. Above all else, they understand this key fact very well: You can't truly get to know the strengths and weaknesses of the candidates if you do not side with them and see them as allies but rather sit across them and see them as opponents or subjects. Great recruiters also understand, no matter how much you strive for excellence in time management or reporting, if you can't truly get to know your candidates you can't recommend or recruit the best fits for the job.

There is a mass trend of automation across all sectors that has been ongoing for a few decades. Repetitive, low value tasks are constantly being replaced by automation and programming, and this won't stop, but only accelerate. When it comes to recruiting, most aspects of the job; be it the candidate search, interview, scheduling, reporting, preparing long and short lists, personality inventories and other aspects; are going to be automated. The hardest to automate part of a recruiter's job is the candidate dialogue and the interview. Thus we can infer, it is where the recruiter generates the highest value. It is, indeed at the core of the job and it is what gives the job its meaning. *So, side with the candidate, know where the value is created and know that the interview dialogue where the recruiter can act as a consultant is at the core of recruiting.*

Key Takeaways

- Prioritize getting to know the person over filling the job vacancy.

- During the interview, focus only on the dialogue.

- Clearly communicate the message you are there to guide and help, not to judge and pick. The candidate should not see you as a threat, but as someone who has a very good grasp of how recruitment works and knows what the opportunities in the organization are.

- Be aware of the dangers of alienation and other business pressures; bring back your focus and motivation through curiosity and a sense of meaning.

The Descent - Principle 6: Know Yourself

Your judgment is **flawed.** So is everyone else's.

The only way to becoming more objective while measuring the competencies of a candidate during an interview or passing judgment in any situation, is to face with this plain and simple fact: Your judgment, as everyone else's is, flawed. Your evaluations are far from objective.

Being a better judge of character and more objective is only possible through:

- Knowing your own values
- Discovering your own biases
- Making an active and sustained attempt at breaking your taboos
- Checking for your own prejudices regularly and systematically

You might rightly ask why it is so hard to be objective. The essence of the matter is we see the world through our own subjective perceptions and we are in a way, stuck in a reality of our own making. Within the bounds of that perception lives our ideas, values and feelings. It is therefore a great challenge to reach a perfect level of objectivity when it is about understanding the inner world of another human being. We can only scratch the surface of this philosophical question regarding the nature of our perception of reality, in what attempts to be a practical guide. So let's limit the analysis to its bare minimum that can allow us to make practical determinations relevant to recruitment.

Different Visions of the World

It is only natural, after all, that we should have different visions of the world. Experience is subjective, memory is fallible. We strive for coherence in our own stories of the world and stories of ourselves but precisely this need for coherence and the act of creating stories means we are filling holes; interpreting, guessing and ignoring some information while adding others.

The classical debate discusses weather it is nature or nurture what molds the human character. We know with more certainty every day, that it is both. What psychologist call genetic temperament has a role in how we react to the world but it is not the only factor that determines behavior. Behavior is determined by the relation, interaction and cumulative reaction of both (genetics and environment) to each other (Cynthia Garcia 2014). This magical mix of random variables in genes and environmental conditions work in a feedback loop, **making** us. And we then immediately go on to **remake** ourselves through what we perceive as our idea of self, intellect and constructed vision of a coherent identity.

Here comes the unsolvable conflict: Our behavior is a (sometimes imperfect) representation of the values we hold. They correspond with our behaviors that express them. Traditional values for instance are closely tied with hedonism, power, universalism; while self-direction values relate with security, conformity and achievement (Anat Bardi 2003). Values are a reflection of ideas we believe to be the right way of behaving. Excluding the situations in which we are in moral or personal conflict, the identity we idealize and the person whom we chose to be is strongly related with the values we hold high. They also happen to be the values through which we judge others. Our way of seeing the world acts as a building block of our character. In turn, the nature of our character influences how we keep on seeing the world. In this character-building process, qualities that we find to be repulsive or unfavorable are left out, while we put greater value in the qualities that we think to be advantageous or desirable. In essence, our character–thus our subjective way of looking at the world–is a unique combination of our genetic traits and the values we believe in. Of course, what we value and how we act aren't always in full synchronization. Everyone can name a few undesirable qualities they hold, but even in that case, there is a quite clear recognition of the difference between the desirable qualities (what the person values and believes to be right) and the undesirable actions (what the person believes to be wrong, but does anyway). In the end, the value system of the person remains intact and in harmony with their personality and worldview. To exemplify, Roccas et al. puts forward that "...Agreeableness correlates most positively with benevolence and tradition values; Openness with self-direction and universalism values; Extroversion with achievement and stimulation values; and Conscientiousness with achievement and conformity values" (Sonia Roccas et al. 2002).

The key implication for interviewing practice is this. *Our own character is indestructibly bound by the values we believe to be right.* The notion of complete objectivity in a given situation (be it a job interview or an argument with a spouse) is as likely as all the humans of the world having the identical character. Complete, perfectionist, water-proof objectivity is impossible, simply due to our human nature. So how do we make the best of what we've got? I suggest an approach, that makes peace with our subjectivity, simply by acknowledging it and reminding ourselves of our nature in every instance where we need to be more objective.

As Good As It Gets: Workarounds for Objectivity

Know your own values. This is an introspective journey each person must take-on by themselves. It is about much more than being a good recruiter. This is about maturing the worldview you have, coming to understand your own culture and your culture-centric, ethno-centric, gender-centric, power-centric values. It is about coming to the recognition where and with which people you grow up have huge effects on your worldview. The move to adulthood, what I mean by a maturation of the worldview, is a healthy process each of us must live. Many of the values we hold are inherited by society, family and cultural environment. Coming to define and analyze these is a first step in a long journey. So before we start thinking about and commenting on other people's values, goals, priorities and choices, we have the moral and ethical responsibility to recognize the subjective nature of ours. We have to recognize our perspective is a relative one. Not the one and only correct way of looking at the world. It is only one of many. Besides, this opens the door to seeing the world through someone else's eyes, which in turn creates the necessary basic conditions for figuring out the personality and competencies of the candidate. So this recognition is not only an ethical responsibility but also a factual advantage towards being better at seeing through people and discovering top talent. Use personality inventories on yourself, get in the candidate seat for a change and ask a recruiter friend of you to interview you, meet with colleagues from around the world and discover what they do and how they think differently.

Discover your own biases. The logical following step after coming to define your values is, to discover the underlying biases you hold. Ask yourself, and be honest with yourself. Are you biased towards people based on the way they dress, the way they choose to display their religion, the way they chose to display their sexual orientation, the way they use their accent? Not only these, but is it possible you have been favoring extroverts over introverts all these time, or that you were a victim of the Halo Effect, generalizing your positive impressions into other areas of the person's character you are trying to understand? As I have tried to make crystal clear, we all hold biases. Discovering them is an important step. Look around you and think of your friends, try to paint a general picture of their shared values. Then look what values are missing in that picture. You might have very determined people all around you, but not as many generous friends (or vice versa). Is it possible you have been focusing very hard to see determination in people you interview, but neglect looking at to see if they are generous?

Make an active and sustained attempt at breaking your taboos. This requires an open mind, and a huge amount of courage! Taboos are by their definition accepted by the peer groups that surround you, and being in conflict with a taboo automatically endangers your status and inclusion within that group. So it is indeed risky thinking from a group psychology perspective. But this is after all, what becoming a truly mature adult is about. Consider you are living in a society or a social setting which is highly intolerant of ambiguous gender identity. To be able to fairly evaluate and truly connect with a candidate who might exemplify such mixed gender behavior; you yourself have to come into the interview having broken your own taboos.

Check for your own prejudices regularly and systematically. This is more about repetition than anything else. Learning what is right and correct is not enough for us, distracted humans. We need to remind ourselves what we have learned constantly and regularly, to make ideas into habits. This is why in every interview the recruiters or the hiring managers must specifically take some mental time off; go back to their observations and cross-check them with their own prejudices. They need to ask themselves the harder questions: "Am I effected by the fact that this candidate looks older than expected?", "Am I drifting towards a more positive judgment because the candidate looks nice and speaks in an overly-confident manner?", "Am I prone to seeing the candidate in a more positive light because he is the last in line and I have to add a name to that short-list today?", "Am I making generalizations because the candidate speaks with a thick accent?"

Being relatively objective is possible, but it takes honesty and hard work.

Key Takeaways

- Our judgment is flawed; complete objectivity is non-existent.
- Each of us holds different visions of the world that is consistent with our values.
- To become more objective and limit our biases, we have to make peace with our subjectivity.
- Workarounds for objectivity:
    - Know your own values.
    - Discover your own biases.
    - Make an active and sustained attempt at breaking your taboos.
    - Check for your own prejudices regularly and systematically.

The Descent - Principle 7: Let Them Know

The two talked for almost an hour.

He asked the questions. She told her life story. Where she was born, how she grew up, her first school and future aspirations, her education at the university.

She told him about her expectations, her first job, what it taught her, how it made her feel. She told about her career desires and aims, other jobs, unaccomplished dreams and wishes. She has gone into a lot of detail about the events that led to her resignation from her previous organization. She told, in detail, what motivates her, what breaks her spirit.

She told about the kind of time she wants to spend during the day, and what kind of vocation gives her meaning. She told about the kinds of people she likes to work with and how she can contribute the organization—what skills she can offer.

She was anxious to know more about what impression she left, and what awaited her following the interview. It was her dream organization after all. She felt she worked very hard to get here and deserved the job. She had also done her best to be as cooperative and transparent as possible.

She waited.

The recruiter said—at the end of the barrage of well-thought out questions—"Olivia, thank you for the chat, it has been nice meeting you. We will let you know our decision in the following weeks," and said no more.

He stared back at her for a moment, and then finally made a gesture to signal the interview was over.

The seventh and final principle of the Pinnacle Method is: Let Them Know. In other words, *inform, be transparent and build long-term relationships*. Every principle laid out so far in this model has been justified by the direct business effects it creates. The case here is not different. Although meeting a recruiter who is transparent, who goes in detail and gives much sought after information might satisfy the candidates, this is only half the reason why letting candidates know details is a good idea. The other half is about organizations' very necessary need to build long-term relationships with candidates to assure they find, recruit and retain the top talent.

The end of the interview does not signal the end of the dialogue. On the contrary, the end of the interview is the beginning of the long term dialogue and human connection between the candidate and the organization. All critical decisions the candidate will make regarding future interviews or even whether or not to work in the organization, will be made after the interview. The state of mind the candidate leaves the interview with and the impression left by the recruiter or the hiring manager will form the foundation of future thoughts about the organization. Remember recruitment is a two-way decision making process. As the recruiter gathers information about the candidate, the candidate will be gathering information about the culture, ethics, values, priorities and strategies about the organization through the recruiter. If and when a final job offer is made, the candidate will look back at the interview experience among other factors and make her decision. Having shared information that is deemed valuable by the candidate and having acted as transparent as possible will go a long way towards a positive and lasting impression. For cases a final job offer isn't made, the candidate experience is still hugely important as it will play a role on the employer brand of the company through social media and word-of-mouth. It is therefore vital to end on a positive note. Ending on a positive note is only possible if the candidate leaves the interview feeling satisfied from the exchange of knowledge rather than exploited.

Let's be meticulous before moving on, and state a fact: Today's corporations are commercial organizations based on information. Information is a perfectly valid currency in the economy we live in. It can be used towards gaining power and/or making a counter move to undermine the power of the competition. Based on this it is easy to see an overall tendency to give out as little information as possible. The recruitment process may sometimes (unfortunately in some limited circles) serve as the stage for gaining strategic information, especially if the company of the interviewee is in the same sector and involved in a competing product sales or marketing strategy. Even in more naive cases, many professionals hesitate about sharing too much information thinking, "better safe than sorry". Looking at both sides of the equation, we can safely deduce information exchange is a sensitive issue.

So when I talk about transparency and informing the candidate, I am well aware of the background and the limitations of the situation. However, it is not all black or white. The simple fact that there needs to be certain barriers for some specific types of information, should not paralyze the recruiters from sharing the information they can. Honestly put, *there is a lot of space between what the candidate can benefit from knowing and the information that shouldn't be shared due to its strategic value.*

Sharing the knowledge in this gray area is–and should be–in the discretion of the recruiter and the hiring manager. Deciding on which information should be kept secret due to its strategic value and which information that can be shared for the benefit of the candidate requires judgment and understanding the business. If and when the interviewer has a strong grasp of the field, she will be able to judge with better accuracy what is okay to share.

So what does the candidate deserve to know? What falls in this so-called gray area of information that does not hurt the strategic interests and competition advantage of the company, but can benefit the candidate?

The recruiter or the hiring manager should, first of all, have a strong grasp of the functional and sectoral area of the company and should be able to narrate the current position of the organization with respect to its competitors and to its target demographic. As mentioned in the previous principles this is not only important to be able to inform the candidate but also to engage in a sector specific in depth conversation when the time comes. A naturally flowing conversation requires knowledge transfer from both parties.

Secondly, the current strategy of the organization should be discussed with respect to the vision it follows. In other words, what is the organization trying to do? What is it trying to ultimately accomplish? Earning more profits and growing is a perfectly valid reason, but this standalone aim is usually a warning sign. It is simply not enough for the meaning seeking prospective employees anymore. In a world of rapidly developing technologies, innovations and with hunger for the newer, fresher, smarter products, every organization that wants grow beyond the average needs to incorporate a vision and ideal. As a recruiter or the hiring manager, you represent the organization to the candidate and as such, should have a very clear mental map of the vision and strategies.

Thirdly, the execution approach and tactical decision making can be discussed as it becomes relevant. Every correct strategy depends on right tactical management but it is not always easy to understand how the top vision shapes middle and bottom level decision making. It is nonetheless very important. Discussing this area with the candidate has the benefit of focusing the discussion from general to specific and finally down to the role itself. Starting at the top level strategy and closing down at the role at each step makes it easier for the candidate to grasp the effect of her future role in the overall organization. A recruiter may go on and on about the responsibilities and duties of the role but it may not make sense to the candidate who is not familiar with the organization specific jargon or the positions of the many functions and departments being talked about. Helping and guiding the candidate to see her future role from a top-down perspective and to understand her potential impact in the organization, accentuates the sense of value bestowed upon the role.

Now that the stage is set, a discussion about the role, the team, the responsibilities and the expectations can take place with assurance that the candidate will have a good apprehension of what she is getting into. As a side note, I see some value in what is commonly referred to as *selling the position* because I think it creates some much needed motivation and flares up the passion a candidate might have. However, *overselling* the position, in other words, exaggerating aspects of the role or displaying the role under a different light as the lead to a different interpretation other than what it really is, can be detrimental. Recruitment process is not the end. It is the beginning of a partnership between the employee and the organization.

Last but not least, the recruiter needs to inform about what the candidate should expect in the following days/weeks. Giving insight into the organizations evaluation strategy of the candidates, the potential next steps and the time frame is always a nice gesture that builds upon the transparency.

So to summarize, going from general to specific– like a funnel, the recruiter should discuss and inform about:

1. The sector, the market conditions, the customers
2. The current strategy, ideals and top level vision of the organization
3. How the top level strategic decision making effects both strategic and tactical execution at middle and bottom levels

4. What effect the role has and where it sits in the organization with respect to the strategy and tactical execution
5. Procedural information

In essence, this is not about methodically lecturing but more about having internalized a culture of openness, empathizing with the curiosity the candidate might be feeling and showing mutual respect more than anything else. Seeing this level of openness from a recruiter cements the candidates' trust, both in the process and the recruiter.

Key Takeaways

- Inform and be transparent to build relationships based on trust.
- See the end of the interview as the beginning of the long term dialogue rather than an end to the conversation.
- Use the space between what the candidate can benefit from knowing and the

information that shouldn't be shared due to its strategic value.

- Have strong and relevant sectoral, strategic, tactical knowledge alongside information about the job and its responsibilities.

Skill Building for Interviewers

The Pinnacle Model you have read through describes how the job interview dialogue should be structured and managed, among other things. It does this with the underlying intention of creating the best possible conditions where the interviewer can make accurate, skillful and authentic observations. Still, the agency of the interviewer is a central determinant for the final insights.

Making the observations themselves, in other words, *connecting the dots* is an imperative and fundamental skill that must be built through study and experience. Without knowledge of the dynamics of the human character and lacking insight into how the human mind works, the conclusions at the end of the interview will be scattered, vague and superficial.

Apparent from the design of this book; learning, or more specifically *skill building* relies on as much theory as practice. The practice is best acquired through the act of real-life interviewing itself. As a recruiter or a hiring manager conducts more interviews, there will be more space for development. The role and necessity of earning field experience needs no further emphasis, it is basically common knowledge.

What is greatly lacking, however, is a study of the theory. Relying only on experience without understanding the theory is like trying to operate on a patient with a dull knife.

I firmly advocate the idea that every professional involved in recruiting needs to know more about the fundamental building blocks of human character and society.

Theories of Personality (with focus on the cognitive, cultural and developmental aspects); **Personality Factors** (with focus on Big Five Traits, 16 Personality Factors and the logic behind their polarity); **Motivation** (with focus on understanding why people do what they do);

Self-actualization (with focus on Maslow's Hierarchy of Needs); **Pattern Recognition** (with focus on how we remember what we remember, use of language, free associations during interviews and recognition of facial features); **Learning Theories** (with focus on Bandura's Social Learning and Skinner's Conditional Learning); **Mirroring** (with focus on how sympathy and empathy occurs); **Signifiers of Mental Capacity** (with focus on the ability for conceptualization and abstraction); **Individualism vs. Collectivism**; **Ethno-centrism**; **Social Stratification** and basics of **Socioeconomics** are among the chief topics that needs to be conquered. In other words, if I were tasked with drafting a curriculum for a class of future recruiters, these areas of learning would be the first to appear in the syllabus.

These areas of learning are the keystones of a healthy and refined worldview. What's more, they are *imperative* for being more than simple observers that rely on gut feeling and becoming 'human analysts' that use theory and behavioral sciences in generating their insights.

I wholeheartedly recommend a study of these core building blocks to anyone with aspirations to not just be good, but great in recruiting.

CONCLUSION

Hiring and retaining top talent is key to organizational success. The Pinnacle Model offers a unified and consistent way of making this possible by approaching the candidate dialogue and managing the interview within a brave new model. It takes advantage of the fact that the recruitment interview is a creative process in which both parties are actors in the creation of a unique dialogue. The dialogue and existence of a Naturally Flowing Conversation is possible to the extent the dialogue is creative, and genuine. Instead of seeing the candidate as the subject whose competencies and characteristic qualities are there for the taking of the interviewer, *The Pinnacle Model sees the interview as a spontaneous, creative, imaginative and collaborative process* where both parties contribute to the dialogue.

The model's core proposition is to add value to any organization, recruiter or hiring manager through offering rare insight into the mind and psychology of the candidate. Going beyond a simple analysis of the candidates' mental world during the interactions, the method here provides a structured and adaptable way of conducting interviews that maximizes the interviewers' ability to figure out the characters, competencies and cultural fits of those who are interviewed. The model owes its robustness to being built on as much theory as practice. It is a culmination of professional field experience, psychological insight and social theory.

The Ascent, The Pinnacle and The Descent come together to describe a complete theory of the candidate and recruiter/hiring manager that is based on interaction psychology. The seven principles shared here are not independent of one another. They are complementary parts of a holistic model that works better if understood rather than memorized. Instead of listing down simple actions that need acting out during the interview, the model introduced was built on central ideals and ideas about identity, the way we construct stories about our self and the way we interact with people whom we have just recently met.

As the final word, the technological revolution we are experiencing now and how it will restructure the recruiting practice in the future should be addressed. The major trends that should be obvious to anyone working closely with technology are automation, digitalization, mobilization and changing structure and importance of networks. Considering all these, it is safe to say some major parts of the job description pertaining to recruitment will change (as is the case for all jobs). The way recruiters network and search candidates have already been revolutionized by Linkedin, that started as a professional networking platform but now evolved into something much bigger with its tools for recruiters, publishers and businesses. Candidate relationship management systems are forming an industry of their own, helping digital record-keeping of past data and adding value with reporting and analytics tools. New systems track and inform applicants, send out automatic replies and give vital information better than the recruiter could do in the past. The only process that is wholly dependent on human interaction is the interview itself. As discussed in the opening chapters, the basic act of understanding the perspective of a human being can only be done by another, as it requires empathy and the ability to shift perspective. Even the interview itself is replicable to some degree with high definition audio and visual telepresence systems; and can be complemented with recorded video interviews before or after the meeting. Still, the main structure of the dialogue and the model laid out here should remain valid and relevant in the future as long as there remains the need to get to know and understand people before doing business with them.

HAND GUIDE & Summary of Key Takeaways

The Ascent - Principle 1: Enable Mental Comfort

- Time pressure causes stress. The interview is a time to slow down, relax and take your time.

- A relaxed candidate will be more honest, the mental and emotional mood of the interview should be led by the interviewer.

- Fear and comfort can't co-exist. Fear is triggered by potential threats. Discover what is perceived as a threat from the candidate's perspective and openly address them.

- Show sincerity and warmth.

- Match the candidate in trait, tone and tempo of thought and speech to the best of your abilities.

Notes:

The Ascent - Principle 2: Earn Respect

- Fight for the respect of the candidate. Do not take it for granted.
- Show you have a very strong grasp of the candidate's field of expertise.
- Keep humility in check, but prove yourself as someone who can discuss specifics, who has technical or intellectual depth.
- Talk about what's hot, share a vision, inspire and impress the candidate.

Notes:

The Ascent - Principle 3: Surprise (Pattern Break)

- Understand how habits work in the structuring of mental models and consequently in interview dialogues.

- Understand how repetition and routine may work against the authenticity sought after in an interview.

- Break thinking patterns and habits through the use of wit, creativity and curiosity.

- Use your ability to structure the interview and determine the content of the questions to your advantage and surprise the candidate. Change the routine with the way you open up the dialogue, with the questions you ask, with the way you address. Let the candidate know this isn't just another interview, where she can get away with pouring out memorized answers.

Notes:

The Pinnacle - Principle 4: Show Genuine Interest

- Recruiting is one of the best careers for inherently curios people; if you are not a curious person, there is little chance you can be a great recruiter.
- In an interview, always be curious; not always about what the candidate is saying– the content, but also in many instances about who the candidate is–the personality.
- Make sure to have fun and enjoy the conversation.
- Shift perspective, make the interviewee feel understood.
- Theorize.
- Mind the cognitive traps.

Notes:

The Descent - Principle 5: Side with the Candidate

- Prioritize getting to know the person over filling the job vacancy.

- During the interview, focus only on the dialogue.

- Clearly communicate the message you are there to guide and help, not to judge and pick. The candidate should not see you as a threat, but as someone who has a very good grasp of how recruitment works and knows what the opportunities in the organization are.

- Be aware of the dangers of alienation and other business pressures; bring back your focus and motivation through curiosity and a sense of meaning.

Notes:

The Descent - Principle 6: Know Yourself

- Our judgment is flawed, complete objectivity is non-existent.
- Each of us holds different visions of the world that is consistent with our values.
- To become more objective and limit our biases, we have to make peace with our subjectivity.
- Workarounds for objectivity:
    - Know your own values.
    - Discover your own biases.
    - Make an active and sustained attempt at breaking your taboos.
    - Check for your own prejudices regularly and systematically.

Notes:

The Descent - Principle 7: Let Them Know

- Inform and be transparent to build relationships based on trust.

- See the end of the interview as the beginning of the long term dialogue rather than an end to the conversation.

- Use the space between what the candidate can benefit from knowing and the information that shouldn't be shared due to its strategic value.

- Have strong and relevant sectoral, strategic, tactical knowledge alongside information about the job and its responsibilities.

Notes:

WORKS CITED

1. Anat Bardi, Shalom H. Schwartz. «Values and Behavior: Strength and structure of relations.» *Personality and social psychology bulletin 29.10*, 2003: 1207-1220.

2. Blackman, Melinda C. «Personality judgment and the utility of the unstructured employement interview.» *Basic and applied social psychology*, 2002: 241-250.

3. Boserup, Ester. «Population and technological change: A study of long-term trends.» 1981.

4. Bozionelos, Nikos. «When the inferior candidate is offered the job: The selection interview as a political and power game.» *Human Relations 58.12*, 2005: 1605-1631.

5. Carl Rogers, Abraham Maslow. *Information Theory.* eM Publications, 2008.

6. Chilisa, Bagele. *Indigenous research methodologies.* Sage Publications, 2011.

7. Cynthia Garcia, Elaine L. Bearer, Richard M. Lerner. *Nature and nurture: the complex interplay*

of genetic and environmental influences on human behavior and development. Psychology Press, 2014.

8. Grey, CGP. *Humans need not apply.* https://www.youtube.com/watch?v=7Pq-S557XQU, 2015.

9. Harter, Susan. *The development of self-representations.* John Wiley & Sons Inc, 1998.

10. Jeanne Meister C., Karie Willyerd. *The 2020 Workplace.* HarperAudio, 2010.

11. Lucas, Suzanne. *25 weirdest job interview questions of 2012.* Moneywatch: http://www.cbsnews.com/news/25-weirdest-job-interview-questions-of-2012/, 2013.

12. Macan, Therese. «The employment interview: A review of current studies and directions for future research.» *Human Resource Management*, 2009: 203-218.

13. Miller, Brian. *How to magically connect with anyone.* https://youtu.be/D4cV8yfgNyI, 2015.

14. Murray R. Barrick, Jonathan A. Shaffer, Sandra W. DeGrassi. «What you see may not be what you get: relationships among self-presentation

tactics and ratings of interview and job performance.» *Journal of Applied Psychology 94.6*, 2009: 1394.

15. Ola Bergström, David Knights. «Organizational discourse and subjectivity: Subjectification during process of recruitment.» *Human Relations 59.3*, 2006: 351-377.

16. Raymond Catell, Herbert W. Bernard, Maurice M. Tatsuoka. *Handbook for the sixteen personality factor questionairre (16 PF)*. Institute for Personality and Ability Testing, 1970.

17. Rifkin, Jeremy. *The end of work*. Social Planning Council of Winnipeg, 1996.

18. Rosen, Sherwin. «Specialization and human capital.» *Journal of Labor Economics* (Journal of Labor Economics), 1983: 43-49.

19. Sonia Roccas et al. «The big five personality factors and personal values.» *Personality and social psychology bulletin 28.6*, 2002: 789-801.

Made in the USA
San Bernardino,
CA